1999/2000
Edition

Anchorages

Along The
Intracoastal Waterway

Skipper
Bob

Best anchorages, free docks, marina and fuel prices from the Hudson River to Key West, including the Delaware and Chesapeake Bays, New Jersey Intracoastal Waterway, Intracoastal Waterway from Norfolk to Key West, Okeechobee Waterway, and the Gulf Coast of Florida from Tampa to Marathon and in the Keys.

Library of Congress Number 99-72100

ISBN 0-9662208-3-8

Anchorages Along the Intracoastal Waterway is the 4th
Edition published by the author based on the publication
Anchorages Along the Intracoastal Waterway originally
published by the Wilmington Power Squadron from 1986
to 1995.

Publications By Skipper Bob

Cruising the New York Canal System: Depth and height restrictions. Lock locations and characteristics. Where to stop. What to expect. Places to stay at no charge with water and electric. Free pump outs! Includes the Erie, Oswego, Cayuga-Seneca, and Champlain Canals. All the information to enjoy cruising the New York Canal System. ISBN 0-9662208-5-4 **$10**

Cruising Comfortably On a Budget: Living and cruising on a boat in the coastal waters of the Eastern United States. What kind of boat to buy, how to outfit it, where to go and stay, and how to live comfortably all on a budget. Tips on saving thousands of dollars while cruising the East Coast, Great Lakes and the Inland water system. Information on cruising the Intracoastal Waterway, Bahamas, and Canada. ISBN 0-9662208-2-X **$24**

Anchorages Along The Intracoastal Waterway: Best anchorages, free docks, marina and fuel prices from the Hudson River to Key West, including the Delaware and Chesapeake Bays, New Jersey Intracoastal Waterway, Intracoastal Waterway from Norfolk to Key West, Okeechobee Waterway, and the Gulf Coast of Florida from Tampa to Marathon and in the Keys. ISBN 0-9662208-3-8 **$14**

Marinas Along the Intracoastal Waterway: Fuel prices, transient slip fees, long term slip fees, do-it-yourself yards, and haul out fees. Mile by mile list of hundreds of marinas from the Hudson River to West Palm Beach. Information on courtesy cars, propane, shopping, CNG, approach depth, number of transient slips, phone numbers, approach directions and much more. ISBN 0-9662208-0-3 **$14**

The Great Circle Route. Cruising the Great Circle Route up the East Coast, across the Great Lakes, down the Mississippi and Tenn-Tom Canal to the Gulf Coast, and across the Gulf Coast to Florida. What charts and cruising guides you need. How to schedule the trip, what to expect and when and where to go. Everything you need to plan this exciting voyage. ISBN 0-9662208-4-6 **$18**

Cruising the Rideau and Richelieu Canals. How to plan a summer cruise on the exciting Rideau and Richelieu Canals of Canada. What charts and guides to get, costs to expect, where to stop and when to go. Complete guide on this exciting trip, which includes stops in Ottawa and Montreal, Canada. Includes historical information, description of the waterways, routes to follow, and much more. ISBN 0-9662208-6-2 **$10**

To obtain copies of the above publications, make out a check or money order to Skipper Bob in US dollars for the amount shown after the publication plus **$2** shipping and handling **for each book**. (Canadian Customers send $3 US for shipping and handling) Send order to: Skipper Bob, 802 Seventh St., ~~Uk St. H~~ PA 17331

802 Seventh St.,
E. Rochester, PA 15074
Ph 724-775-5892
SkipperBob@Worldnet.att.net
Http://SkipperBob.home.att.net

Sources For Skipper Bob Publications
(North to South)

Canada:
   The Nautical Mind, 249 Queen's Quay West, Toronto, ONT M5J 2N5, Ph 416-203-1163
   Upper Deck Marine Store, 2 Clarence St., Kingston, ONT K7L 5H8, Ph 613-542-2292
Washington:
   Armchair Sailor, 2110 Westlake Ave, North, Seattle, WA 98109, Ph 206-283-0858
Rhode Island:
   Armchair Sailor - Seabooks, 543 Thames St., Newport, RI 02840, Ph 800-29CHART
New York:
   Wardell Boat Yard, 1 Sweeney St., North Tonawanda, NY 14120, Ph 716-692-9428
   Ports of Pittsford Gifts, 7 Schoen Place, Pittsford, NY 14534, Ph 716-383-9250
   The Boating Center, 400 W Commercial St, East Rochester, NY 14445, Ph 800-942-2583
   Lift Bridge Book Shop, 71 Main St., Brockport, NY 14420, Ph 716-637-8354
   Erie Canal Museum, 318 Erie Blvd East, Syracuse, NY 13202, Ph 315-471-0593
   The River's End Bookstore, 19 W Bridge Street, Oswego, NY 13126, Ph 315-342-0077
   Ess-Kay Yards, Inc., PO Box 68, Brewerton, NY 13029, Ph 315-676-2711
   Waterford Canal Center, 65 Broad Street, Waterford, NY 12188, Ph 518-235-1547
   Hop-O-Nose Marine, Inc., PO Box 389, Catskill, NY 12414, Ph 518-943-4640
   Riverview Marine Services, Inc. 103 Main St., Catskill, NY 12414, Ph 518-943-5311
Maryland:
   Fawcett Boat Supplies, Inc., 110 Compromise St., Annapolis, MD 21401, Ph 800-456-9151
   Spring Cove Marina, PO Box 160, Solomons, MD 20688, Ph 410-326-2161
Virginia:
   WT Brownley Co., 118 W Plume Street, Norfolk, VA 23510, Ph 757-622-7589
North Carolina:
   Inland Waterway Treasure Co, PO Box 797, Oriental, NC 28571, Ph 800-249-7245
   Scuttlebutt, 433 Front St., Beaufort, NC 28516, Ph 252-728-7765
   West Marina, (Wrightsville Beach) 1994 Eastwood Road, Wilmington, NC 28403
South Carolina:
   Harborwalk Books, 723 Front St., Georgetown, SC 29440, Ph 843-546-8212
   JJW Luden & Co., Concord at Charlotte St., Charleston, SC 29401, Ph 803-723-7829
   Downtown Marina, 1010 Bay St., Beaufort, SC 29902, Ph 803-524-4422
Georgia:
   Palmer Johnson Marina, 3124 River Drive, Savannah, GA 31404, Ph 912-356-3875
Florida:
   Municipal Marina, 111A Avenida Menedez, St. Augustine, FL 32048, Ph 904-824-9300
   Titusville Municipal Marina, 451 Marina Road, Titusville, FL 32796, Ph 407-269-7255
   West Marine, 1509 Harbour Ave, Melbourne, FL 32935, Ph 407-242-9600
   Bluewater Books & Charts, 1481 SE 17th St., Ft Lauderdale, FL 33316, Ph 954-763-6533

INTRODUCTION

This publication is a compilation of information received from boaters. It covers the Hudson River, New Jersey Intracoastal Waterway, Delaware and Chesapeake Bays, Intracoastal Waterway from Norfolk to Key West, Okeechobee Waterway and the West Coast of Florida from Tampa to Marathon.

The primary intent of this publication is to furnish information on anchorages. To this end, all anchorages identified in the covered area are listed, with pertinent information about that anchorage. A detailed explanation for the format used in listing anchorages is contained at the end of this introduction, but includes protection from wind, holding, tidal range, scenic beauty, wake protection, ease of shopping and amount of current in anchorage.

Marinas are not generally listed. The average cost for a transient to stay in a marina on the East Coast varies by area from a high of $1.43/foot per night on the Hudson River to $0.78/foot per night on the Okeechobee Waterway. For detailed information on marinas from the Hudson River to Fort Lauderdale, FL., refer to *Marinas Along the Intracoastal Waterway*. To aid those boaters who are trying to stay within a budget, limited information on marinas which charge $0.75/ft or less is shown.

Diesel fuel prices vary throughout the area covered. The average diesel fuel price on the East Coast fell nearly $0.06/gallon between June 1998 and June 1999. The highest average diesel fuel price is found on the Hudson River at $1.30 per gallon. An in depth survey of marinas and fuel prices between the Hudson River and Fort Lauderdale, FL was conducted in June 1999. Appendix 1 is a list of the average and lowest diesel fuel prices I found in each area of this book. Inexpensive fuel stops are found about every 200 miles and most cruisers can save significant dollars by patronizing these stops. For a complete list of marinas surveyed and their fuel prices, refer to *Marinas Along the Intracoastal Waterway*.

Prices found in this book were current at the time of publication and to the best of my knowledge. However, all **prices are subject to change without notice**.

Some locations within the area covered provide courtesy or free dockage. Wherever encountered, this service is listed. A list of do-it-yourself yards can be found in appendix 2 of this book. For a complete list of do-it-yourself prices, see *Marinas Along the Intracoastal Waterway*. Bridges that open, and all locks, are listed with height and time restrictions.

Boaters are encouraged to send me information, which will substantiate, improve, add to, or change information already contained in this publication. Comments must be received before 1 July each year, to be included in that years revision. The new edition each year will be published about August 1st. Those individuals who contribute significantly to each new revision will be sent a courtesy copy of the new publication. Skipper Bob will make decisions as to what will be included and who contributes "significantly". Please include your name, the name of your boat, the vessel type, length and draft. A current list of contributors is shown on page 82. Send all information to Skipper Bob, PMB463, 1150 Carlisle Street, Hanover, PA 17331.

How to Read This Guide

The first number in special brackets, such as "{4.2}", is the average spring tidal range in feet. Bare in mind, that this is only the average, not the extreme. The effects of wind and severe weather will change this number dramatically and should be taken into account.

When a number appears in brackets after a bridge it represents the clearance under that bridge at high water. "(7')", would indicate that under normal tide conditions there is a 7-foot clearance at high water under that bridge. Remember that spring tides, wind, and severe weather can change the amount of clearance you find under any bridge. **Before** you get too close to a bridge, check the bridge clearance before trying to go under the bridge. Then, if necessary, request an opening.

Before three years ago, all bridges and locks on the East Coast responded to VHF Channel 13. In 1997 Florida bridges switched to VHF Channel 09. In 1998, South Carolina bridges switched to VHF channel 09. To assist the boater, I have listed the VHF Channel which each bridge and lock responds to behind the bridge or lock name in bold letters. "**-VHF 13**"

A six-digit number appears in brackets in the introduction to any anchorage, dock or marina. This number represents the value of that location, with "4" being the best and "1" the worst. The categories rated are holding, wind protection, current flow, wake protection, scenic beauty, and ease of shopping; in that order. An anchorage with a rating of "(432441)" would be interpreted as follows: This location has excellent holding, good wind protection, fair currents in the range of .5 to 1 knot, excellent wake protection, pristine scenic beauty, and no shopping in the area. For ease of use, an Anchorage Rating Code (ARC) table is provided on the next page. In addition, an ARC reminder is printed at the top of each page in this book.

At the end of each listing a notation <u>may</u> be made in brackets. This notation indicates that someone made a comment on that entry in the last year. As an example, "(#12)", would indicate that contributor #12 sent in a comment on that listing this year. Entries of more than one number, i.e. "(#12, 15) indicate that two or more cruisers commented on that entry. Listings with no entry in brackets behind them were not verified this year. A listing of contributors is provided on page 88.

It is important to note that the **information contained herein is not to be used for navigation**. Prudent boaters will use the current charts, appropriate navigation aids, recent notice to mariners, and electronic navigation equipment while operating their vessel. The most recent changes on the waterways due to shoaling, sunken vessels, etc. cannot be and will not be found in this publication.

Anchorage Rating Code (ARC)

1st Digit - (X-----) Holding:
> 4 - Excellent, Usually sand or clay or tied to dock
> 3 - Good, usually mud or mooring ball
> 2 - Fair, possibly some weeds, rock, or hard to set
> 1 - Poor, may have stumps, weeds, sunken obstacles, soupy

2nd Digit - (-X----) Wind Protection
> 4 - Excellent, protected from all directions
> 3 - Good, protected from 180-360 degrees
> 2 - Fair, protected from 45-180 degrees
> 1 - Poor, no protection, flat land or open water

3rd Digit - (--X---) Current Flow
> 4 - Excellent, less than .2 knot
> 3 - Good, currents of .2 to .5 knot normal
> 2 - Fair, currents of .5 to 1 knot normal
> 1 - Poor, currents of more than 1 knot

4th Digit - (---X--) Wake Protection
> 4 - Excellent, little traffic
> 3 - Good, enforced no wake zone, but lots of traffic
> 2 - Fair, limited traffic
> 1 - Poor, big wakes from big ships, or from lots of traffic

5th Digit - (----X-) Scenic Beauty
> 4 - Excellent, pristine beauty, no development
> 3 - Good, little development, natural beauty
> 2 - Fair, lots of controlled development
> 1 - Poor, run down or overdeveloped

6th Digit - (-----X) Ease of Shopping
> 4 - Excellent, walk to near by shopping
> 3 - Good, short dinghy ride to good shopping
> 2 - Fair, short dinghy ride or walk to few stores
> 1 - Poor, no shopping in the area

Example: (444321)

This anchorage would have excellent holding, excellent wind protection, little if any current, good wake protection, only fair scenic beauty, and no shopping in the area.

INDEX

Hudson River

The Hudson River runs for 155 statute miles in a southern direction from Troy Lock above Troy, NY to the Statue of Liberty in New York Harbor. The Hudson River is deep, has many areas of rocky bottom, and a lot of boat traffic; including ocean going cargo ships. The Hudson River is tidal all the way to Troy and flows at nearly two knots in both directions twice per day. Because of the large amount of traffic, the swift currents, and the rocky bottom, anchoring in the Hudson River can be both a chore and dangerous. Prudent boaters should have charts 12335, 12341, 12343, 12347, and 12348 on board while cruising the Hudson River.

The above referenced charts do not show statute miles. However, I have marked my charts off in statute miles starting with 0 above Troy Lock and ending with 155 just below the Statue of Liberty. To assist you in locating the points I reference by statute mile, I have also referenced these points by Latitude [XX xx.xx], and any name found on the chart; such as town, creek, bay, etc.

Waterford, NY is the Alpha and Omega, the beginning and the end, of a trip up or down the East Coast of the United States. Just two miles above the Troy Federal Lock, Waterford is strategically placed to assist the cruiser. Waterford offers abundant **free docks.** There is a high wall nearly 1000 feet long and just west of the first bridge a 300' long floating dock.

A visitor center located at the free dock provides local and Erie Canal information and sells **Skipper Bob books.** Restaurants, post office, pizzeria, and phone are located within six blocks. Walk 3 blocks north to Route 4 and turn east. Cross the Hudson River to shop at Price

> **Waterford, NY**
>
> Beginning and end.
> Large **free dock.**
> Good place to stock up on food items.
> Visitors center.
> Post Office.
> **Skipper Bob books**

Choppers Supermarket, Burger King, or Hannaford Drug Store. If planning on buying a lot of food, a boat can move from the wall at Waterford across the Hudson River and north 0.1 mile to just below the fixed bridge. On the east bank is a 50' floating dock maintained by Price Choppers 24-hour supermarket. Walk up the steps at the dock and you are the rear of Price Choppers.

Mile 1.0, {5.1}, [42 44.25], Troy, (441322): Troy Town Dock Marina is a 1400' dock along eastern town wall, below Adams Island. Only limited shopping in down town area. Southern 100' of dock reserved as courtesy dock for restaurants. (#1)

Mile 16.6, {5.0}, [42 31.80], Castleton-On-Hudson, (431224): The Castleton Boat Club on the east shore offers a crane for do-it-yourself mast stepping for $30. (#1)

Mile 21.0, {4.7}, [42 28.50], Coeyman, (431322): Courtesy docking for the Muddy River Café is located at the Coeymans Landing Marina on the western shore on a space available basis. (Consult your charts for rock wall near town of Coeyman)

Mile 23.0, {4.5}, [42 26.75], New Baltimore, (431332): Courtesy docking for the Hudson Harbor Steak and Seafood Restaurant is located at Shady Harbor Marina on the western shore on a space available basis. Shady Harbor Marina had diesel fuel for $1.19/gal in June 99. (#1)

Mile 24.5, {4.5}, [42 25.40], Schodack Creek, (434231): Enter the Schodack Creek below Houghtaling Island on the eastern shore. Stay in the center and proceed 1 to 2 miles up river to this very popular anchorage. Anchor in 10-12 feet of water.

Mile 28.3, {4.3}, [42 22.20], Rattlesnake Island, (434332): Enter area behind Rattlesnake Island on south side west shore. North end has been filled in. Anchor in 8-10' at lower end of island.

Mile 29.0, {4.3}, [42 22.00], west of Coxsackie Island, (421232): Enter either north or south of Coxsackie Island. If coming from the south, mind the charts and hug the western shore starting more than a mile below the island. Anchor in 15-20'.

Mile 29.5, [4.3], [42 21.00], Coxsackie, (421224): Small dock available for day time tie up at Coxsackie. Enter either north or south Coxsackie Island. If coming from south, mind the charts and hug the western shore starting more than a mile below the island.

Mile 32.0, {4.3}, [42 19.30], east of Stockport Middle Ground, (333231): Enter from the south side of Stockport Middle Ground Island. Follow the deep water indicated on the chart until close to the eastern shore. Follow the eastern shore north until north of Judson Point. Anchor in 12-15'. The deep water is quite narrow and two anchors are recommended to control swinging.

Mile 35.0, {4.4}, [42 16.25], west of Middle Ground Flats, (421123): Enter the west side of Middle Ground Flats from either the north or south. Anchor north of Murderers Creek in 15-20'.

Mile 37.0, {4.5}, [42 15.50], Athens, (431124): The village of Athens provides 150' of docks for temporary visitors on the western shore of the Hudson River. While overnight tie up is not permitted, you can walk into town for limited shopping.

Mile 41.6, {4.6}, [42 12.40], Catskill Creek: Proceed west up Catskill Creek for the following points of interest:

(1) 0.2 miles on north shore, Mike's Catskill Point Family Dining (443324). Mike's provides 200' of floating dock for dining patrons. Open M-F 4PM to 10PM, S&S from Noon to 11PM. Pizza, steaks, chops, etc. Stay free overnight on dock after meal, if dock is not too busy. (Avoid weekends and holidays)

Hop-O-Nose Marina
Off the Hudson
Quiet peaceful setting
Floating docks
Swimming Pool
Mast stepping
Ships store
Restaurant on site
Skipper Bob books

(2) 0.25 miles on north shore Riverview Marina will step mast for a fee. Supply of charts, guides, fuel, and marine supplies.

(3) 0.5 miles on south shore Hop-O-Nose Marina will step mast for a fee. Supply of charts, guides, fuel, and marine supplies.

(4) 0.6 miles stream, (344422) anchor just past Hop-O-Nose Marina before low fixed bridge. Room for 3 or 4 boats. Stay clear of marina and anchor in 6-8'.

Mile 46.0, {4.5}, [42 09.30], Duck Cove, (334221): Just south of the jetty at Duck Cove, you can anchor in 6-8' below the protection of the jetty. Come in from the south below the G109 buoy and stay at least 100 feet from the end of the jetty.

Mile 52.2, {4.3}, [42 04.60], Saugerties, (344431): Up the Esopus Creek on the western side of the Hudson is one of the best-protected anchorages on the Hudson. Follow the creek until just off the stack and tank on the chart. Do not go beyond this point as the creek gets shallow fast and has a rock bottom. Anchor in 15-20' next to rock face on the northern side of the creek. Avoid the southern side of the creek at this point, as there is a sand bar built up there. Use of fore and aft anchor allows 3 or 4 vessels room to anchor in this protected spot. This anchorage provides excellent protection from strong winds and storms. On weekdays with calm night, don't go back so far, and anchor (434322) in the wide spot in front of marina on south shore. Not as protected, but more air.

Mile 63.8, {4.2}, [41 55.20], Kingston: Proceed west up Rondout Creek for:

(1) Town dock at Kingston (444424): 1.5 miles up Rondout Creek between two fixed bridges on the north side of Rondout Creek behind the small island are the town docks for Kingston. You can carry 8-10' behind the island, and can turn a 40' boat around in the narrow channel. Many short finger piers have been added to their floating dock making it difficult for a larger boat to tie up. There is also a wall before the floating docks where you can tie up without electric. Pay $2 per hour ($3 on weekends and holidays) while you shop or visit the town or museum.

(2) Rondout Creek anchorage, (444421): The best anchorage on the Hudson is located 4 miles up Rondout Creek. Proceed past Gumser Island and anchor south of the channel just before the fixed bridge in 8-10'. Room for many boats. Usually very busy on weekends and holidays.

Mile 77.0, {3.5}, [41 44.30], Roosevelt, (421121): The Hyde Park Marina on the eastern shore provides 200' of courtesy docks for the Brass Anchor.

Mile 78.9, {3.5}, [41 42.80], Highland Landing, (421124): Mariners Harbor Restaurant provides 200' of courtesy docks on west shore above bridge.

Mile 86.0, {3.4}, [41 36.80], Marboro, (4211240: West Shore Marina just above Marboro had diesel fuel for $1.16/gal in June 99. (#1)

Mile 94.5, {3.2}, [41 31.00], Newburgh, (421121): Courtesy docks for a few boats are provided for the River House Restaurant on the western shore at the Newburgh Yacht Club. There is 5' at dockside, and no overnight stays.

Mile 98.0, {3.1}, [41 27.40], Pollepel Island, (421131): The anchorage lies in deep water close to the eastern shore of the Hudson River. Enter the narrow channel ¾ of a mile below Pollepel Island and hug the main land shore as you proceed north to anchor in 8-10' behind the island. This anchorage provides an interesting view of the ruins of the castle on Pollepel Island.

Mile 103.3, {2.8}, [41 23.50], West Point, (431121): **Free Dock.** The large ship terminal at West Point is available to transient boaters if no ships are scheduled. Few ships stop at West Point, and 3 to 4 boats can tie up on the face pier at night. The terminal has large pilings and some skill is required to secure your boat so as to avoid damage due to wakes from passing boats and swift tidal current.. Check with the Dockmaster upon arrival, or call ahead at 914-938-3011, to verify availability of dockage. Do not attempt to tie up on the north or south end of the terminal as cruise boats are normally kept there. Do not attempt to land at either of the floating docks on the wall north of the large terminal as the water is very shallow (about 2') at these docks. While spending the night at West Point, you can visit this historical facility and the military museum located there. There is no shopping for civilians on the base, and the town outside the base is about a 1-mile walk south of the terminal.

Mile 112.0, {3.2}, [41 16.50], Lents Cove, (421122): Guinan's Country Store on the eastern shore is just south of Peekskill, on the northern shore of Lents Cove and provides courtesy docking for patrons.

Mile 119.6, {3.4}, [41 11.50], Haverstraw Bay, (423232): North of Croton Point on the eastern shore you can anchor in 7-10' with fair protection from a south wind. The approach is straight forward; follow the charts.

Mile 122.0, {3.5}, [41 10.30], Croton Bay, (334332): South of Croton Point on the eastern shore you can anchor in 4-5' with good protection from all but a south wind. Stay south of Tellers Point 300 feet as you swing in behind the protection of Croton Point.

Mile 123.0, {3.6}, [41 09.75], Ossining, (421121): The Hudson Riverboat Company provides courtesy slips for those desiring to eat at their restaurant. They are located on the eastern shore 0.4 miles south of Tellers Point and just south of the Shattemuc Yacht Club.

Mile 127.0, {3.7}, [41 04.50], Tarrytown, (421122): The Dockside at Tarrytown provides courtesy docks for customers. They are located 0.1 mile north of the Tappan Zee Bridge on the eastern shore. Look for the Texaco sign. Good place to catch a train to New York City. (#4)

Mile 141.5, {4.3}, [41 52.60], at chart label "Mast", (422221): Englewood Boat Basin State Park on the west bank behind the breakwater had diesel fuel for $1.20/gal in June 99. (#1)

Mile 149.0, {5.2}, [40 46.25], Weehawken, (434412): Arthur's Landing Restaurant provides fine dining with a view of Manhattan. Port Imperial Marina makes slips available for Arthur's Landing on the western bank behind breakwater on a space available basis.

Mile 149.8, {5.2}, [40 45.60], Weehawken, (434412): The Lincoln Harbor Yacht Club on the western shore provides slips on a space available basis while you eat at either the Chart House, Ruth's Chris Steak House, Houlihan's, or the Food Court.

Mile 152.0, {5.3}, [40 43.53|74 01.90], Jersey City, (434424): The Newport Yacht Club and Marina provides slips on a space available basis for lunch and dinner patrons at the Café Newport. The slips are north of the north pier at the west most end.

Mile 153.1, {5.3}, [40 42.75|75 02.55], Jersey City, (434424): The Liberty Harbor Marina, on the western shore, inside the Morris Canal Basin, provides dock space for the Liberty Seafood Restaurant on a space available basis.

Mile 155.0, {5.3}, [40 41.70|74 03.75], Liberty State Park, (334431): Entrance to this designated anchorage is obtained by entering the channel just south of Liberty Island. Go west, following the channel as it zigzags and enter the protected anchorage on the western shore south of Liberty State Park. Anchor in 14-20' close to the Liberty State Park bulkhead. Avoid the area near the breakwater on the south side of this anchorage, as it is shallow. This anchorage provides good protection for all but southeast winds. You will normally find 5 to 10 cruisers at anchor in this anchorage. Some vessels take their dinghies to shore on Liberty State Park at the floating dinghy dock provided at the northwest most corner of this anchorage, but I would not recommend it. This anchorage provides an excellent place to stop after the run up the coast of New Jersey and before starting up the Hudson River. There are no good anchorages for the first 52 miles of the Hudson River, and the strong tidal currents should be taken into account before starting up the Hudson River. This anchorage is a good place to lay over to take the current into account.

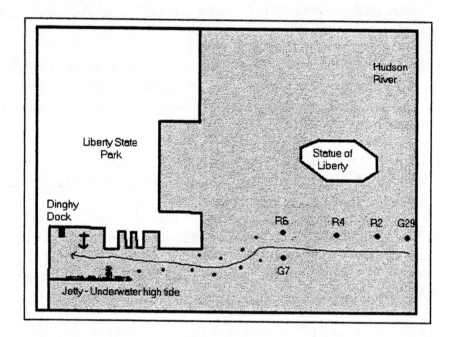

New Jersey Stretch

The New Jersey stretch includes the waters from the Verrazano-Narrows Bridge in New York Harbor, down the New Jersey Coast to the Delaware Bay entrance of the Cape May Canal. This includes the 25 mile open ocean stretch from the Sandy Point to Manasquan Inlet and the 117 mile Intracoastal Waterway trip inside New Jersey from Manasquan Inlet to Cape May Canal inlet on the Delaware Bay. While all cruisers must take the outside route from New York to Manasquan, many do not take the inside route from Manasquan to Cape May due to limited water depth and fixed bridges with low clearance. For those who elect to take the outside route from Manasquan to Cape May, the information on the inside route may still be helpful, particularly where it applies to anchorages or services near the Atlantic City and Cape May Inlets.

Locations on the first stretch from New York Harbor to Manasquan are referenced to by both Latitude and Longitude [XX xx.xx|XX xx.xx] and chart name. Those locations in the New Jersey Intracoastal Waterway are referenced to by statute mile number and chart name.

The stretch from New York Harbor to Manasquan is characteristically deep open water and has only a few places where a boat can seek protection from bad weather or winds. The New Jersey Intracoastal Waterway is very protected, with lots of places to anchor. It is however, very shallow, with many areas of 4-5' at low tide. However, with a 3 foot tide, a boat drawing 5' can easily cruise these waters on a half tide rising.

The bridges with a height greater than 25' are not listed in the New Jersey stretch, since no boat with an overhead clearance greater than 25' should try to take the New Jersey Intracoastal Waterway. The fixed 25' bridge at Great Egg Harbor Inlet restricts this waterway to vessels that can clear this bridge. The closed clearance of bridges with less than 25' are listed for ease of reference.

Boats cruising this section of the New Jersey coast should have the BBA Chart Kit, Region 3, New York to Nantucket and to Cape May, New Jersey, or NOAA Charts 12404, 12324, and 12316.

North Side Lower Bay, {5.7}, [40 32.50|74 08.20], Great Kills Harbor, (334222): Shortly after you leave the Verrazano-Narrows Bridge headed south, there is a protected anchorage to the west. 5 miles south of the Verrazano-Narrows Bridge is the Green can marked "C13" in the Chapel Hill North Channel. Turn due west and head for the Great Kills light 4 miles distance. This light marks the entrance to the Great Kills Harbor and a protected anchorage where you can find protection from any wind direction in 15-20'. (#5)

South Side Lower Bay, {5.6}, Sandy Hook: Behind Sandy Hook are four anchorages:

(1) Sandy Hook, [40 27.90|74 00.60], (423231): Just off the Coast Guard Station offers protection from NE through SW winds.

(2) Horseshoe Cove, [40 26.75|74 00.05], (433241): A little further south it offers protection from all winds but S through SW. Shallower than charts indicate. (#15)

(3) If the winds shift while anchored behind Sandy Hook, try the Navesink River [42 23.20|73 59.40], (441424): A boat can continue south behind Sandy Hook and the Highlands to the Navesink River. Here you can find a protected anchorage north of the #6 marker and east of Upper Rocky Point in 10-12' of water off the county park.

(4) Atlantic Highlands,[42 25.10|74 01.20]: Weather permitting, anchor just south of the Atlantic Highlands Breakwater (323223) near the east end. No mooring balls there, but stay clear of fair way. The nearby Yacht Club has launch, showers, water, groceries nearby, laundry and boating supplies.

Mile 0, {4.8}, Manasquan Inlet, (443414): **Free Dock.** Upon entering Manasquan Inlet, turn hard to Port nearly 160 degrees at the first opening and enter the waters behind the eastern shore. Follow the narrow waterway back past the Coast Guard Station, commercial shrimp boats and cruise ships to the fixed bridge at the entrance to Lake Louise. On the port side, the Shrimp Box Restaurant provides 300' of dockage for patrons. (Closed Monday and Tuesday) Overnight dockage is permitted, no water or electric, and rafting is mandatory. Check in with the Shrimp Box reservation desk. You can pay $20 to stay overnight, or you can spend at least $20 on meals and stay overnight at no charge. It is an easy walk to the ocean boardwalk with all the usual fan fare and several convenience stores. A regular supermarket, and shopping area is a one-mile walk. (#5)

Mile 0.8, {4.6}, The Glimmer Glass, (333433): At R2, turn north into Crabtown Creek and follow the well-marked channel through the Glimmer Glass Bridge. Bear to Port just past green day mark into protected basin. Stay close to northern shore and only 20' off boats in slips. Anchor near the moorings in 6'. Deep water extends about 15 feet past the mooring buoys to the south. Dinghy west to sandy shore by railroad tracks. Follow road north and east to center of town and shopping. Acme supermarket, hardware store, laundry, etc.

Mile 0.9, {4.6}: Hoffman's Marina east of RR bridge had diesel fuel for $1.00/gal in June 98.

Mile 1.0, {4.6}, Brielle Railroad Bridge-**VHF 13** (3'): Usually open if no train scheduled. Lots of train traffic. (#5)

Mile 4.6, {0.4}, Bay Head, Dale Yacht Basin, (424122): On the port side as you exit the Point Pleasant Canal headed south is the Dale Yacht Basin where diesel fuel was $0.94/gal in June 99. (#1)

Mile 4.6, {0.4}, Bay Head Harbor, (444222): After leaving Point Pleasant Canal turn to Port and anchor in basin near Dale Yacht Basin in 6'.

Mile 4.8, {0.4}, Metedeconk River, (444424): For serious shopping, leave the Intracoastal Waterway between markers 2 and 3 and go west up the Metedeconk River 3.3 miles. In the South fork proceed slowly west and anchor in 4-6' as needed. Dinghy to the end of the south fork and tie up to bridge. Two blocks west of the tip of the south fork is a large mall with supermarket, Boat US, West Marine, etc. If you have trouble in the south fork, try the north fork and proceed to Johnson Boat Basin and tie up temporarily at their dock in 5'. The mall is a 4-block walk from Johnson's. (#1,15)

Mile 6.3, {0.4}, Mantoloking Bascule Bridge-**VHF 13** (14'), **Restricted:** Memorial Day to Labor Day, Sat, Sun, and Hol, 9AM to 6PM opens on the hour and every 20 minutes. On demand the rest of the time. (#1)

Mile 9.5, {0.4}, Kettle Creek, (424232): Head northwest from G21 into Kettle Creek. Anchor in 4' for best wind protection. Busy on weekends.

Mile 10.0, {0.4}, Silver Bay, (424232): Head west from mile 10.0 into Silver Bay. Anchor in 5' for best wind protection. Busy on weekends.

Mile 14.1, {0.4}, Seaside Heights South Bridge-**VHF 13** (30'), **Restricted:** (1) No openings Dec 1 to Mar 31. (2) From Apr 1 to Nov 30 Sat, Sun, and Hol from 11AM to 2PM opens on the hour and half-hour. On demand the rest of the time.

Mile 14.7, {0.5}, Toms River, **Free Dock**: There are two places to stay 1.8 miles up the Toms River: (1) On the north side is a public dock (434224) adjacent to Island Heights where you can tie up overnight at no charge if space permits. Room for 5 boats in 5 ½' of water. (2) Exactly opposite on the south side is a small cove (334221) (Cocktail Cove – local name) where you can anchor in 6-8'. (#1,15)

Mile 22.2, {0.4}, Island Beach, (324241): Head 120M from R64A and feel your way in as far as you can go to the south of Tices Shoal. Anchor in 4-5' and dinghy to shore. Walk to beach. Very popular anchorage on weekends.

Mile 25.9, {0.4}, Barnegat Inlet, (433221): Safe anchorage if you are using Barnegat Inlet. Just inside inlet to south in white water shown on charts. South to fuel dock, west to channel opposite several three-story homes. Anchor in cove to north of houses or 200' off land spit running ½ mile north. Depth 6-10'.

Mile 45.5, {2.5}, Long Beach, (431124): Beach Haven Yacht Club on the east bank had diesel fuel for $0.95/gal in June 1999. (#1)

Mile 45.8, {2.7}, Mordecai Island, (344312): Anchor east of Mordecai Island in 6-8'. Enter Liberty Thorofare between markers 104 and 106. Room for 5-10 boats. (#15)

Mile 55.5, {3.8}, Mullica River, (323441): Proceed 6 miles west of the ICW at marker 139 across the Great Bay and up the Mullica River to the first major horseshoe bend at the tip of Blood Point. Anchor in the bend in 15-20'. Deep draft boats can cross the Blood Ditch, but this ditch and the Bass River are heavily traveled by large power boats and should be avoided as an anchorage. The second horseshoe bend before the fixed bridge has the potential of a good anchorage with slightly more wind protection.

Mile 65.1, {4.8}, Atlantic City, (421121): For overnight stops many boats anchor just southeast of fixed bridge. Anchor in white water on charts west of G17. Current is swift and lots of traffic.

Mile 67.2, {4.8}, RT30 Highway Bridge-**VHF 13** (20'): On demand.

Mile 68.9, {4.8}, NJDOT Beach Thorofare Bridge-**VHF 13** (4'): On demand. Pass through on east side. 35' fixed bridge just beyond. (#20)

Mile 70.0, {4.8}, RT40 Inside Thorofare (Albany Ave.) Bridge-**VHF 13** (10'), **Restricted:** Jun 1 to Sep 30 opens on hour and half hour from 9AM to 9PM. Except closed from 4PM to 6PM. On demand all other times.

Mile 71.2, {4.8}, Dorset Ave. Bridge-**VHF 13** (9'), **Restricted:** Jun 1 to Sep 30 from 0915 to 2115 opens on ¼ and ¾ hour. On demand rest of time. (#5)

Mile 71.5, {4.8}, Ventnor City, (444423): Leave ICW just before entering the west end of the canal and anchor in the Ventnor City basin in 6-8'. (#5)

Mile 74.0, {4.8}, Margate City Bascule Bridge-**VHF 13** (13'): On demand. Be patient, toll bridge operator has to walk out to open bridge. (#5)

Mile 75-79, {4.6}, Great Egg Harbor Inlet: The ICW Broad Thorofare was closed in 1995 due to silting behind the Great Egg Harbor Inlet. Now boats have to leave the charted ICW and bypass the Broad Thorofare and cross the Inlet between two bridges. Follow the channel markers carefully. Channel markers change sides in the basin inside the inlet. (#1,5)

Mile 78, {4.6}, Ocean City Longport Inlet Bridge-**VHF 13** (23'): On demand. Signboard reads 2' lower than actual available height. Operators slow to respond, as they must walk out the bridge from the east bank to operate it. (#5)

Mile 80.4, {4.6}, 9th Street Bridge-**VHF 13** (14'), **Restricted**: Memorial Day to Labor Day opens on hour and half hour Sat, Sun and Holiday. All other times, on demand. (#5)

Mile 81.5, {4.6}, Shooting Island: **CAUTION**: Pass close to R264. Green side shoals sharply. (#1)

Mile 86.6, {4.6}, Railroad bridge: Destroyed and partially removed.

Mile 102, {4.8}, Stone Harbor Bridge-**VHF 13** (11'): **Restricted: Memorial** Day to Labor Day, 8AM to 5PM, on the hour and every 20 min thereafter. On demand the rest of the time. (#20)

Mile 105.2, {5.2}, North Wildwood Bridge: Replaced by high bridge.

Mile 108.8, {5.3}, Post Creek Basin: Do not attempt to anchor in this basin on the east side of the ICW. Although the chart shows 10-22', there is only 3' at low water.

Mile 108.9, {5.4}, Wildwood (R47 or Rio Grand) Bridge-**VHF 13** (25'): On demand. (#20)

Mile 109.0, {5.4}, Wildwood, (431224): Schooner Island Marina had diesel fuel for $0.90/gal in June 1999. (#1)

Mile 109.1, {5.4}, Ephraim Island, (342312): east of the ICW just south of the Wildwood Bridge anchor between the new floating marina and Ephraim Island in 8-10'. The south end of Sunset Lake usually has a lot of small jet boat activity which makes it less than desirable as a place to anchor. (#1)

Mile 112.1, {5.4}, Lower Thoro, (331112): East of the ICW enter Lower Thoro and anchor in 18-20' near a dilapidated green/white metal building. Reported crowded on weekends. (#1)

Mile 112.2, {5.4}, Two Mile Beach Bridge-**VHF 13** (23'): On demand.

Note - Vessels northbound should go outside if they draw more than 5' or require a clearance of more than 25'.

Mile 113.5, {5.5}, Cape May, (321113): Anchoring south of the ICW near the Coast Guard Station is possible, but not recommended for overnight. The wakes and currents make this an uncomfortable place to spend the night. It is a good place to anchor to visit the community of Cape May. For overnight, proceed north to mile 109.1 or 112.1. (#15,18)

Mile 115.1, {5.5}, Cape May Railroad Bridge: Destroyed and partially removed. (#5)

Chesapeake and Delaware Bays & C&D Canal

The stretch from Cape May, NJ includes the Delaware and Chesapeake Bays and the C&D Canal. Of course the greatest portion of this guide is dedicated to the Chesapeake Bay. Swift currents and exposed waters with few protected anchorages mark the 55-mile trip up the Delaware Bay. For most cruisers, the Delaware Bay is a one-day adventure, hopefully in good weather. The 207-mile trip on the Chesapeake Bay on the other hand, has many anchorages and ports of call. The tidal current on the Chesapeake Bay is not nearly as swift as on the Delaware Bay and there are many tributaries on the Chesapeake Bay where one can cruise in the worst weather.

I have marked my charts of the Delaware Bay, C&D Canal and Chesapeake Bay with statute miles. The Delaware Bay follows the ship channel from 0 at Cape May to 55 at the C&D Canal. The C&D Canal goes from mile 0 at its eastern end to mile14 just west of the high bridge at Chesapeake City. Finally, the Chesapeake Bay starts at mile 0 at the northern most end at the bridge at Chesapeake City and increases to mile 204 at ICW mile 0, Hospital Point, Portsmouth, VA.

To plot the most direct route down the Chesapeake Bay and follow the statute mile markers I have placed on my chart follow these instructions. Mile 0 is just west of Chesapeake City high bridge in the C&D Canal. Proceed in the ship channel 12 miles southwest passing Turkey Point. Continue following the ship channel to mile 38.4, G11, the entrance to Baltimore Harbor Channel. Continue southwest in the ship channel, passing under the Chesapeake Bay bridge at mile 49.5, to R2 at mile 54, the entrance to Annapolis, Severn River. South from R2 in the ship channel to mile 99.7 at Cedar Point. From Cedar Point, follow the ship channel south and southeast to mile 138.3 at R62, off Ingram Bay. The shortest route down the bay leaves the deep ship channel here and follows the magenta line south from R62 to Thimble Shoal at mile 191.8. From Thimble shoal follow the most direct route into Norfolk and Hampton Roads and then down the Elizabeth River to mile 207 of the Chesapeake Bay and mile 0 of the ICW.

To aid cruisers on the Delaware Bay, C&D Canal, and Chesapeake Bay all entries in this book reference the statute mile markers outlined above as well as Latitude and Longitude, and the chart name.

Before cruising the Delaware or Chesapeake Bays obtain a copy of the appropriate charts. I recommend the BBA Chart Kit, Chesapeake and Delaware Bays, Region 4. In addition, anchorages on the Chesapeake Bay abound and only the most prominent ones used by vessels traversing the most direct north/south route are listed. For more detailed information on cruising the Chesapeake Bay refer to *Chesapeake Bay Magazine's Guide to Cruising The Chesapeake Bay*, or the Waterway Guide, Mid-Atlantic Edition.

Delaware Bay

Mile 34.0, {6.0}, [39 20.70|75 22.00], Cohansey River, (332241): Once committed to the Delaware Bay, the Cohansey River is your best bet to wait out bad weather or currents. West bound, pass Ship John Shoal light in the ship channel and proceed about 1 mile before turning NE towards the Cohansey River entrance. Well-marked and deep, follow the Cohansey River until you find a wide spot and anchor in 15-25'. Best anchorage is after the first sharp turn to the west. (#15,28)

Mile 50.7, {6.0}, [39 30.53|75 34.33], Reedy Island, (321231): 4.3 miles south of the entrance to the C&D Canal at G3R head 290M towards the south end of Reedy Island. Enter anchorage between G1 and R2 between Reedy Island Dike to the south and Reedy Island to the north. Anchor behind Reedy Island in 7-20'. In SW to N wind anchor close to shore opposite the church spire in 17-20'. Great spot for overnight, or after transiting the C&D Canal. (#15)

Mile 54.0, {4.6}, {39 35.00|75 29.50], Salem River, (331322): Leave ship channel just north of "WR10R" and follow Salem River channel 4.5 miles to anchor in 7-10' in large bend behind north of the island cut off by Salem River channel. Short dinghy trip up river to Salem for supplies.

C&D Canal

Mile 7.8, {2.6}, Conrail Lift Bridge-**VHF 13** (45): Normally up unless train is coming. (#1)

Mile 8.5, {2.6}, [39 32.70|75 42.60], Summit North Marina: This marina in the basin on the north side of the canal had diesel fuel for $0.89/gal in June 99. (#1)

Mile 13.7, {2.6}, [39 31.60|75 48.60], Chesapeake City: Entrance channel to basin recently dredged in 1998. The basin offers two means to wait for weather and or tides on the Delaware Bay or to rest after crossing: Also, visit the C&D museum while here.
(1) Anchor (344423) in the east end of the basin in 8-10'. (#5)
(2) **Free Dock,** (444224): The 200' wall on the west end is available for free overnight docking. (#5)

Mile 13.9, {2.6}, [39 31.70|75 48.70], Chesapeake City: Schaefer's Marina had diesel fuel for $0.89/gal in June 99. (#1)

Chesapeake Bay

Mile 8.0, {2.4}, [39 28.20|75 55.00], Bohemia River, (234232): On Eastern Shore, enter the Veazey Cove on the Bohemia River. Popular anchorage.

Mile 12.8, {2.4}, [39 33.72|75 58.32], Northeast River: Three inexpensive marinas (444412) lie up the Northeast River. Round Turkey Point from G 7 staying south of GR C "ER". Follow the Northeast River channel up the west shore of Elk Neck 11 miles to the protected waters of the Northeast River. Charlestown Marina to the NW of R12 was $0.75/ft. East of R14 in Ford Run on the north bank is McDaniels Yacht Basin with a rate of $0.70/ft. On the south bank of Ford Run is Northeast Yacht Sales with a transient rate of $0.60/ft. All rates current in June 1999. (#1)

Mile 18.0, {1.8}, [39 22.20|75 58.90], Sassafras River, (344331): On eastern shore of the Chesapeake Bay off Sassafras River, south of Ordinary Point, enter Turner Creek. Deep water close to western shore. Relatively free of sea nettles. (#8,15,25)

Mile 28.0, {1.6}, [39 16.30|76 12.60], Fairlee Creek, (333332): On Eastern Shore of the Chesapeake Bay southeast of R36 enter Fairlee Creek. Watch for strong current at well-marked entrance. Anchor further in, in 5-6'. (#15,25)

Mile 30.7, {1.6}, [39 17.50|76 23.10], Middle River, (433421): West 7.7 miles from R32 at 306M brings you to the entrance marker R4 at Middle River. Pass Bowley Bar to Starboard and turn north into Galloway Creek. Anchor past Bowley Quarters Marina in 8'. Can dinghy to marina, but no shopping in area.

Mile 38.4, {1.3}, [39 09.40|76 15.40], Swan Creek, (344323): On the Eastern Shore, follow the channel in and anchor north of R10. Dinghy dock at Haven Harbor Marina.

Mile 38.4, Enter mouth of Patapsco River headed west for Baltimore:
  (1) 6.0 miles west, {1.2}, [39 07.60|76 27.50], Bodkin Creek, (344322): Enter Bodkin Creek, proceed around day mark R12 and anchor between Goose Cove and Jubb Cove in 9'. (#5,25)
  (2) 17.7 miles west, {1.2}, [39 16.70|76 34.80], Canton, (434333): Anchor on the north shore between the two marinas next to high rise building in 10-12'. Dinghy to wooden dock on shore and tie up on side of dock, not dock face. (Used by water taxi) Safeway across street and West Marine two blocks east. (#1)
  (3) 19.3 miles west, {1.2}, [39 17.10|76 36.70], Baltimore Inner Harbor, (344323): Anchor in 30' just off World Trade Center building. Small place. Very busy on weekends. Visit the National Aquarium, Harbor Place, or Maryland Science Center. (#4,15)

Mile 42.3, {2,1}, [38 58.15|76 14.70], Kent Narrows, (441224): Free **Dock.** The Crab Deck restaurant provides 15 slips for dinner patrons. During the week, when not crowded, vessels that stop for dinner are normally permitted to stay overnight at no charge. Located on east bank just south of drawbridge. (#1)

Mile 44.0, {2,1}, [39 12.30|76 03.70], Chestertown, (343423): On eastern shore enter Chester River and proceed 15 miles up river to anchor off town in 8-10'. River carries 10' all the way in the channel. Town offers charming collection of 18th century architecture. Crowded by permanent moorings. (#8,25)

Mile 45.0, {1.0}, [39 04.80|76 27.50], Magothy River, (434331): Enter well marked Magothy River on western shore and follow Gibson Island shore north to protection offered behind Dobbins Island in 7-10'. Very shallow near island. Crowded on weekends. Even better protection in small coves north of Gibson Island. (#25)

Mile 52.0, {1.0}, [39 00.00|76 27.40], Mill Creek, (334222): 2 miles south of Bay Bridge, head NW and enter Mill Creek off Whitehall Bay. Many good anchorages, select the best wind protection and relax.

Mile 54.0: Head northwest from R2 to the Severn River, and the Annapolis area. A major boating center with many marine supply stores. Annapolis has extensive sightseeing, including the Naval Academy.

    (1) Lake Ogleton, {1.0}, [38 56.90|76 27.80], (334322): On the south side of the Severn River at marker G1. Follow marked channel and select your anchorage where room permits in 8-10'. A quieter anchorage, but somewhat away from hustle of Annapolis.

    (2) Back Creek, {1.1}, [39 58.05|76 28.60], (334323): Due west of R8 is the entrance to Back Creek. Anchor in 8-9' where space permits. Close enough to dinghy to shore for just about anything. (#5,15)

    (3) Annapolis, {1.1}, [38 58.55|76 29.00], Spa Creek, (434123): City provides moorings for $15 in the area just north and south of Bascule Bridge on Spa Creek. Showers $1. Some adventurous souls anchor in the exposed area off the Naval Academy wall, but I do not recommend it. Water taxi to town available or dinghy to dock at end of Market Slip (a.k.a. Ego Alley) on west side of mooring field. Tie up to mooring ball and pay dockmaster on Market

Slip or wait and he will come by. (#4,25)

(4) Annapolis, {1}, [38 58.55|76 29.00]: Annapolis City Marina, Ltd. On eastern bank before Spa Creek bridge had diesel fuel for $0.81/gal in June 99.(#1)

(5) Spa Creek, {1.1}, [38 58.40|76 29.20], (344323): Proceed up Spa Creek past Bascule Bridge and city moorings and anchor where room permits anywhere in the next ½ mile in 8-10'. Dinghy to Dead End Street in Spa Creek or the dock at end of Market Slip just north and west of Bascule Bridge. (5,18)

Mile 59.6, {1.1}, [38 52.60|76 31.10], Rhode River, (334222): On western shore enter Rhode River and pick your spot either just west of R4 or south of High Island and west of G7. Water skiers can be a problem.

Mile 67.6, {1.2}, [38 44.40/76 19.10], Dun Cove, (334331): On Eastern Shore enter Harris Creek from north (mile 67.6) via Knapps Narrows and from south via Choptank River (mile 81.4). Give Seth Point a wide berth to starboard. Anchor west of Seth Point in 8'. If crowded, go further up Harris Creek to Waterhole Creek.

Mile 67.6, {1.2}, [38 43.00/76 20.80], Knapps Narrows, (441224): Knapps Narrows Marina on Eastern Shore had diesel fuel for $0.76/gal in June 1999. (#1)

Mile 67.6, {1.0}, [38 43.70/76 32.60], Herring Bay, (324232): On western shore 5.5 miles from the normal north/south route, Herring Bay makes a good anchorage in a westerly wind. Tuck in under the high bank about halfway between R2 and the cliff and anchor in 12'. (#15)

Mile 81.2, {1.6}, [38 34.70|76 04.40], Cambridge: Two inexpensive marinas can be found 20 miles up the Choptank River at Cambridge. The Gateway Marina (444421) across the river was $25 a night. Yacht Maintenance Company (444424) was $0.50/ft and is located on the Port as you enter Cambridge Creek. There is also an excellent anchorage (444223) inside Cambridge Creek just before the drawbridge on the Starboard. Anchor in 9' in basin near Shell fueling point. Dinghy ashore for good shopping.

Mile 81.4, {1.6}, [38 32.40|76 14.80}, Hudson Creek, (334431): A good place to stay 1/3 the way from the C&D to Norfolk. On the Eastern Shore enter the Little Choptank River and then Hudson Creek, and anchor north of Casson Point. Use caution entering Hudson Creek. Follow course from a point midway between Choptank G7 and G9 to Hudson Creek. For north wind, anchor south of Cedar Point on the Little Choptank. (#18)

Mile 97.5, {1.3}, [38 19.20|76 27.40], Solomon's Island Area, (334323): Enter the Patuxent River and then the main harbor at Solomon's Island on the north shore. Anchor in any of several spots, depending on needs and weather. Anchor in main harbor just past gas docks on left, Back Creek near G5, in Mill Creek, in Old House Cove, etc. On Back Creek: Zahnhizer's Marina accepts trash for a modest fee. Holiday Inn allows use of dinghy dock for $1/day. Shopping center 1 block from Holiday Inn. Maritime Museum (worth visiting) has a dinghy dock for use while visiting museum. Spring Cove Marina at the end of Back Creek on port had diesel fuel for $0.80/gal in June 1999. (#1)

> **Spring Cove Marina**
>
> Last marina on western shore of back creek.
> Well-stocked ships store.
> Swimming pool.
> Close to town (easy walk).
> Low fuel price.
> Full service boat yard
> 410-326-2161
> **Skipper Bob books**

Mile 106.2, {3.6}, [38 21.89|75 36.00], Salisbury, (444424): An inexpensive marina, well off the normal north/south route, 46 miles from the north/south route up the Wicomico River on the eastern shore to Salsibury. The Port Of Salisbury Marina was $0.50/ft in Jun 98.

Mile 122.0, {1.4}, [37 59.60|76 28.70], Glebe, (334431): On the southern shore a short way up the Potomac River, The Glebe, west of marker R8 on the Coan River, is somewhat off the normal north/south passage, but a good place to hole up.

Mile 122.0, {3.0}, [38 52.30|77 01.30], Washington DC, (334221): A trip up the Potomac River on the western shore is well worth it, if you have the time. Allow at least a week. You can anchor in the Washington Channel, dinghy ashore and be within walking distance of the mall, monuments, Capitol, White House, etc. Note - Woodrow Wilson Memorial Bridge-**VHF 13** (50'), **Restricted:** Closed 5AM to midnight Mon to Fri and closed 7AM to midnight Sat, Sun, and Hol. (#15)

Mile 129.2, {2.1}, [37 53.40|76 14.20], Smith Point, (434331): Follow the shallow channel (6') west into the Little Wicomico River. Anchor on north side between R6 and G7 in 6-7'. Many crab pots. (#15)

Mile 136.0: Enter the Great Wicomico River on the western shore for 4 different stops:
(1) Cockrell Creek, {1.3}, [37 50.70|76 16.90], (334112): Cockrell Creek is not generally recommended as an overnight anchorage due to fish processing plant with its associated odor and fishing fleet. However, there is an anchorage just past the docks of the Cockrell Creek Seafood Company. Good seafood can be had at the seafood counter or small sandwich type restaurant. Try the crab cakes! (#21)

(2) Sandy Point, {1.3}, [37 49.50|76 18.60], (333231): Sandy point offers a good anchorage a short way off the north/south path for all but NW winds. Plenty of room and good depth. With the lighted buoys, this anchorage can be accessed at night.

(3) Horn Harbor, {1.3}, [37 51.30|76 20.60], (344431): Horn Harbor offers a very protected anchorage for those bad nights. Be careful negotiating the entrance and anchor in comfort in 6'. Excellent seafood restaurant just up river from anchorage open except Tuesday from Memorial Day to Labor Day. Reasonable food prices.

(4) Mill Creek, {1.6}, [37 47.55|76 19.50], (444331): Alternative to Sandy Point. Follow well-marked channel giving G3 and R4 a wide berth. Go upstream at least ½ mile. Anchor in 15'. (#2,3)

Mile 139.0, {2.4}, [37 58.60|75 71.90], Crisfield, (344322): On the Eastern Shore enter Somers Cove Marina basin and anchor in 10'. Dinghy to marina to obtain services in small town. Excellent crab dinners in all restaurants. Sea Mark Marina past the entrance to the basin on starboard offered exposed transient slips for $10. Somers Cove Marina had Diesel for $0.79/gal in June 99. (#1)

Mile 142.0, {2.6}, [37 42.55|75 45.50], Onancock Creek, (344433): Follow Onancock Creek upstream 4.5 miles to town of Onancock and anchor in bight on red side of channel or in north fork at town. Channel is well marked. Can carry 7' to anchorage. Dinghy to marina and restaurant. Short walk to town for supplies.

Mile 143.2, [2.4}, [37 43.70|75 55.00], Snow Hill, (442424): **Free Dock;** To visit historic Snow Hill head almost due east from RW"RP" on north/south route about 15 miles to R2 at the entrance to the Pocomoke River. Follow the marked channel 45 miles upstream to the sleep community of Snow Hill. Tie up at Sturgis Park on the starboard just before the lift bridge in Snow Hill. Water and electric. No charts beyond Williams Point and day mark G23. Water is deep bank to bank beyond this point to Snow Hill.

Mile 146.0, On the western shore Fleets Bay has three good stops:

(1) Indian Creek, (A): Pitmans Cove, {1.3}, [37 41.50|76 21.25], (344431): Follow the well-marked channel up Indian Creek to G11. Turn to Port and follow the channel in until the channel breaks to Starboard. Follow the channel back another couple hundred yards. Anchor in total protection in 6-8'. (B) Rappahanock Seafood, {1.3}, (424212): Halfway to the Chesapeake Boat Basin on the north side of Indian Creek is the Rappahanock Seafood with 8' along side. You can stop to eat at the small restaurant or purchase fresh seafood. Or anchor in the little creek just past the restaurant. They are open 7 days a week. (#21)

(2) Dymer Creek, {1.3}, [37 40.10|76 19.80], (334441): Follow marked channel and proceed north from G7 and anchor in 8-10' behind Grog Island. (#25)

(3) Antipoison Creek, {1.3}, [37 38.00|76 21.80], (444441): Follow channel
through little bay up Antipoison Creek beyond wharf for a secluded and
well-protected evening. (#21)

Mile 152.6: On the western shore enter the Rappahannock River and proceed up river 6
miles to the entrance to Broad Creek on the south bank. Walden's Marina was
$0.75/ft + $3.00 electric, 1st marina on west side. Norton Yacht Sales was
$0.75/ft, 3rd marina on east side. J&M Marina was $0.50/ft + $5.00 for electric,
4th marina on west side. June 99. (#1)

Mile 152.6: On the western shore enter the Piankatank River for 2 different stops. This
river is about 2/3 the way down the bay and is a very popular place to stop when
transiting the north/south route:
(1) Fishing Bay, {1.4}, [37 32.00|76 20.50], (323232): This anchorage is 10 miles
west from the north/south route past the first peninsula on the north side.
It is easier to get into than Jackson Creek, but less protected. More
exposed for those buggy nights with a good breeze, but no strong wind.
Some places are soft mud and/or grass and poor holding. Anchor in
Fishing Bay for north winds and move south to Godfrey Bay for south
winds.
(2) Jackson Creek, {1.4}, [37 32.60|76 20.00]: Good stop 7.5 miles from
north/south route, near Deltaville, VA. Follow chart and day marks
carefully on entering. Channel is deep, but shoals quickly outside
channel. 4 possible stops:
(A) Anchor (334432) in south branch in 6-8' just beyond public dock.
(B) **Free Dock:** (434424) Public dock on starboard, if space available.
Short walk to good hardware store and post office. Two miles to
West Marine.
(C) Anchor (334432) in north branch in 6-8' just past marina. Watch for
shoal shown on chart extending from north shore between north
and south branch. Two miles to grocery. (#5)
(D) Yacht Club, {1.4}, [37 32.60|76 20.00], (434431): Fishing Bay Yacht
Club on Jackson Creek on southern branch allows 1 day free tie up
to recognized yacht club members and has activities most
weekends. Members often run visitors into town for supplies. (#5)
(3) Edward's Creek, {1.9}, [37 29.30|76 17.60], (344331): Enter Milford Haven
on south side of Piankatank River. Do not use Hole-In-The-Wall entrance
from Chesapeake Bay unless you have local knowledge. This channel
changes constantly. Edward's Creek offers good protection in 6-8'.
Watch for strong currents at entrance to Milford Haven near marina.

Mile 172.0, {2.9}, Mobjack Bay:

    (1) Put-In-Creek, [37 25.00|76 20.30], (334333): Enter Mobjack Bay on western shore and proceed up the East River to Put-In-Creek. Anchor in 8-10' with good protection. Short dinghy ride to end of Put-In-Creek and the town of Mathews for reasonable shopping.

    (2) North River, [37 25.00|76 27.00], (334341): Enter Mobjack Bay on western shore and proceed northwest and enter North River. Follow the North River past the turn to the west and anchor just before the river turns north to the south of Elmington Creek. You will pass some of the most beautiful old Tidewater Virginia estates. Secluded and scenic. (#21)

Mile 177.0, {2.4}, [37 16.00|76 10.00], Cape Charles, (444324): On the Eastern Shore is a quaint stop with protected waters at Cape Charles. Follow the well-marked channel up into the Harbor Basin. Proceed to the "Harbor of Refuge" in the NE corner and tie up for $10 per night. (#6)

Mile181.0, The York River on the western shore offers two stops of interest to cruisers:

    (1) Sarah Creek, {2.8}, [37 15.50|76 28.30], (344332): Proceed 15 miles west to Sarah Creek. Anchor opposite Yachthaven Marina fuel dock and covered slips. Sarah Creek is too shallow to enter. While a good way off the north/south route, it is a good place to visit Yorktown, Jamestown, and Williamsburg. Anchor beyond Yachthaven marina and arrange rental car through them.

    (2) Chisman Creek, {2.8}, [37 11.00/76 25.00], and (334231): For an overnight stop a short way off the north/south route use Chisman Creek. Turn NW off Poquoson River at R14 and proceed up Chisman Creek to anchorage that suits you. Also anchorage in Poquoson River south of R16 is OK but, more open to wind/waves.

Mile 191.8, Turn east towards the mouth of the Bay for two anchorages:

    (1) Little Creek, {3.1}, [36 55.40|76 11.10], (334121): Offers very well marked entrance channel off Chesapeake Bay. Limited anchorage in bight to starboard as you enter Little Creek. Proceed ¼ mile past first marina. Can accommodate two or three boats in about 8' near an old ferry wreck on beach. Cobb's Marina, (444324) 1st on port, offers an inexpensive stop at $0.75/ft (Boat US –25%). (#1,4)

    (2) Broad Bay, {1.0}, [36 54.25|76 02.45], (323331): The last anchorage before you leave the Chesapeake Bay headed east into the ocean. 2 miles west of the Bay Bridge Tunnel enter and follow channel markers carefully. Stiff tidal current under Lessner Bridge (clearance 39') and up Long Creek. (Long Creek has strictly enforced 5-knot speed limit). Anchor in Broad Bay 300' south of Seashore State Park in 8'. Crab pots are good indicator of limits of good water.

Mile 196.2: After reaching Norfolk, there are two places to stop just off Hampton Roads:
(1) Hampton River, {3.1}, [37 01.10|76 20.50], (343323): Follow channel north from Hampton Roads to Hampton River and Hampton, VA. Anchor in 8-10' on Hampton University side (east) opposite Visitor Center, or south of Hampton Yacht Club just above junction of Sunset Creek, or for a quarter mile above the bridge to the east side of the channel. Dinghy landing OK at Downtown Hampton Public Pier floating docks on east side of river adjacent to Radisson Hotel and Visitor Center. Radisson Hotel happy hour provides cheap dinner Monday through Friday. Tour Fort Monroe by City Bus or arrange for tour of Virginia Air & Space Museum. (#7)
(2) Willoughby Bay, {3.1}, [36 57.50|76 17.10], (324211): Enter Willoughy Bay from Hamton Roads following the north or south Channel. Anchor east of Willoughby Bay Marina in 10'. Lots of airplane noise all day starting early in the morning. Willoughby Bay Marina on the north shore had a transient rate of $0.75/ft in June 99. (#1,15)

Mile 203.4, {3.2}, [36 54.40|76 18.50], Lafayette River, (334321): The last stop before entering the Intracoastal Waterway headed south. Follow channel 1.2 miles from Elizabeth River up Lafayette River. Anchor south of channel near R14 in 6-8' just before first bridge opposite Norfolk Yacht and Country Club.

Mile 206.8, {3.2}, Hospital Point: End of Chesapeake Bay and beginning of the Intracoastal Waterway at mile 0.0.

Intracoastal Waterway, Norfolk to Miami

The Intracoastal Waterway (ICW) from Norfolk to Miami is a series of rivers, bays and lagoons connected by man made canals to form a protected waterway from Norfolk to Miami. The bottom is generally either mud or sand with few if any rocks. Because the entire waterway is tidal, the boater encounters currents and changing water levels, that must be accounted for during navigation. There are many good anchorages, and some which are down right unpleasant, if not dangerous.

Before traveling on the ICW, obtain all the necessary charts. We have found that the BBA Chart Kit, Norfolk, VA to Jacksonville, FL Region 6 and the BBA Chart Kit, Florida East Coast, Including the Keys, Region 7, to be more than adequate.

The above referenced chart kits show mile markers for the entire ICW. All references to anchorages bridges, marinas, etc. will refer to the mile marker, starting at 0 in Norfolk, and ending at mile 1089 at Miami Beach Marina, Miami, FL. In addition, names found on the charts will be included, where available.

Bridges and locks from Norfolk to Florida monitor either 13 or 09. To assist you, I have included the VHF channel used by all locks and bridges immediately behind their name. Bridges with restricted openings may not respond. Schedules are usually posted on or near the bridge. The closed vertical clearance for the bridges that open is shown in parentheses behind the bridge name. In addition, most bridges have a "clearance board" beside the bridge that shows the current closed clearance based on actual water height at the time. Always check this board before trying to go under a closed bridge. Be aware you may have to add 2, 3, or 4 feet to the clearance shown on the board. That is because some bridges show "low steel clearance" and you have more room at the center of the bridge. This information is usually shown on the "clearance board".

Deadheads (water soaked logs) can be found from time to time all along the ICW. They are frequently stirred up by passing boats and for this reason alone, you should not follow too closely to large or fast moving powerboats.

The color of day markers may change sides as the ICW crosses different channels and rivers as it runs north and south. Just remember that a small yellow triangle or square is painted on each ICW marker and these small day mark symbols will stay on the same side at all times when going north and south. Look for them on the larger red and green day marks and make sure they are present when following the channel.

Mile 0, {3.3}, Hospital Point, (333122): To the west of the channel, anchor in 8-10'. Room for 20+ boats. Numerous crab pots at times. Convenient to ICW, though not the most pleasant anchorage. When heading south, leave by 5:50AM to beat bridge restrictions. This will get you past the Steel Bridge by 7AM. (#2)

Mile 0.5, {3.3}, Portsmouth, (444124), **Free Dock**: On the west side of the ICW in the Ferry Basin, tie up on the 200' south wall. No charge for overnight, but not recommended as a stay. The wakes of passing vessels rock the boat very hard in this basin. It is a good place to stop, hit the ATM, visit Portsmouth, grocery ½ mile, etc. Sign warning of two-hour limit is largely ignored.

Mile 0.6, {3.3}, Portsmouth, (444224), **Free Dock:** On the west side of the ICW in a second basin called "High Street Landing", tie up while shopping in Portsmouth. Sign posted says "No Overnight" but is largely ignored for vessels arriving late and leaving early. (#1)

Mile 2.6, {3.2}, N&PBL RR Lift Bridge-**VHF 13** (6'): On demand, usually open. (#5)

Mile 2.8, {3.2}, Jordan Lift Bridge-**VHF 13** (15'), **Restricted**: Closed 6:30AM to 7:30AM and 3:30PM to 5PM excluding holidays. On demand all other times. (#5,20)

Mile 2.9, {3.2}, Jordan Bridge, (444314): **Free Dock,** on the east side of the Jordan Bridge, south of the toll station. Line up on the range marks and head straight in to the 100' fixed dock. Room for 3-4 boats just before boat ramp. One-mile walk east to post office, convenience store, florist, fast food, Chinese restaurant, and auto parts store. (#3)

Mile 3.6, {3.2}, Norfolk Southern RR Bridge-**VHF 13** (10'): On demand, usually open.

Mile 5.8, {3.2}, Gilmerton Bridge-**VHF 13** (11'), **Restricted**: Closed M-F 6:30AM to 8AM and 3:30PM to 5PM excluding holidays. On demand all other times. (#2,5,20)

Mile 5.8, {3.2}, Norfolk and Southern RR Bridge-**VHF 13** (7'): Usually open when no train is scheduled. (#5)

Mile 7.3: The point where you must decide whether to take the scenic Dismal Swamp Canal, or the more direct and well traveled Virginia Cut route. Call the US Coast Guard on VHF Channel 22 to see if the Dismal Swamp Canal is open. Sometimes it is closed due to lack of water.

Dismal Swamp Route

The Dismal Swamp route should have at least 6' of water. It is the prettier of the two routes and offers more and nicer places to tie up at no charge, than the Virginia Cut.
The Dismal Swamp Canal has two locks; both operating on restricted hours. Because of the restricting locks and speeds in the canal, most of the fast sport fishing boats and powerboats take the Virginia Cut route. That alone makes the Dismal Swamp route a pleasure for trawlers and sailboats.

Mile 8.5, {3.0}, Deep Creek basin, (444341): A short distance along the Dismal Swamp Canal you pass a man made basin on the southern side. 8' at the entrance, it deepens to 20' in the middle and offers an excellent anchorage. Expect lots of boats on weekends and holidays. (#1,15)

Mile 10.5, {3.0}, Deep Creek Lock, (344431): If you arrive after the last locking at 3:30PM, you can anchor just north of the lock. Anchor on the west side of the channel or tie to one of the pile clusters on the west side. It gets shallow very quickly west of these pile clusters. You will be in a good position for the first opening at 8:30AM the next morning. Expect company. Usually 3 or 4 boats there each night.

Mile 10.6, Deep Creek Lock-**VHF 13**, **Restricted:** Locking at 8:30AM, 11AM, 1:30PM, and 3:30PM. Lift 8'. Deep Creek Bascule Bridge (4') operates in conjunction with lock. (#5)

Mile 11.0, {0.0}, Deep Creek, (444424), **Free Dock**: Room for two boats to tie up to east wall, with 11' alongside, just south of Deep Creek Bridge. Adjacent to small shopping mall on east side with fast food, Chinese restaurant, hardware, auto parts store with some marine supplies, and Food Lion. On the west side Ekard Drug and 7-11. (#1)

Mile 21.5, {0.0}, Lake Drummond Feeder Ditch, (444411): Room for one boat to tie up at each of two small wooden docks on the east bank north and south of the feeder canal. Take your dinghy to Lake Drummond. Day stop only. Small boatlift will lift your dinghy to level of Lake Drummond.

Mile 28.0, {0.0}, NC Welcome Station, (444431), **Free Dock**: Room for 4 or 5 boats to tie up at the 150' wall on the east bank provided by the NC Welcome Station. Public rest rooms, water, showers and telephone available. Rafting expected. Welcome station closed on Mondays. Pick up free North Carolina Coastal Cruising Guide. (#2,5,15,17)

Mile 32.0, {0.0}, South Mills Bridge-**VHF 13** (4'), (444424), **Free Dock**: Tie up to east or west bulkheads south of bridge. Bridge opens in conjunction with south Mills Lock. Convenience and auto parts store as well as restaurant (5AM to 1PM) close by. Gulf station couple of blocks east will take waste oil. No place to tie up south of lock. There is a limited space to tie up just north of the bridge on the east or west wall while waiting for the bridge/lock to open. (#5)

Mile 32.5, South Mills Lock-**VHF 13**, **Restricted**: 8' drop. Locking at 8:30AM, 11AM, 1:30PM, and 3:30PM. (#5)

Mile 43, {1.5}, Goat Island, (244431): Anchor in 6-7' anywhere behind Goat Island.

Mile 46.7, {1.5}, NS RR Bridge (3'): No radio. Usually open if no train scheduled. If closed sound horn.

Mile 50.7, {1.5}, Elizabeth City Bridge-**VHF 13** (2'), **Restricted:** Closed 7AM to 9AM and 4PM to 6PM, except for opening at 5PM. On demand rest of time. (#24)

Mile 50.6, {1.5}, Elizabeth City, (444324): The Thorton Development Corp. maintains 10 slips with water and electric. They are the first slips on the west bank when south bound after going through bridge. The overnight fee is $15 paid on the honor system. (#15)

Mile 51.0, {1.5}, Elizabeth City, (424224), **Free Dock**: 14 slips provided by city for up to 48 hours for transients. Rest rooms next door at Water Works. Walking distance to restaurants and hardware. Short cab ride (1.5 miles) to shopping malls and grocery stores. Rose Buddies will host wine and cheese party if more than 4 boats. If slips are full you can tie up to Mariner's Wharf one block south even though the signs say "no docking". (Overflow permitted) Slips exposed to SE wind and are not pleasant in strong SE wind. (#5)

Virginia Cut Route

The Virginia Cut offers faster passage for vessels than the Dismal Swamp Canal since there is only one lock and only a few speed restrictions. The Virginia Cut is more developed on the north end and shopping is more extensive in Great Bridge. The marinas offer more marine services on this route.

The single lock is used primarily to control the tide height difference between the Albermarle Sound and the Chesapeake Bay, rather than raise a boat over an obstacle.

Mile 8.1, {3.2}, N&PBL RR Bridge: Removed May 97 (#5)

Mile 8.8, {2.5}, Steel Bridge-**VHF 13** (12'), **Restricted**: Closed M-F, 7AM to 9AM and 4PM to 6PM. On demand on Federal Holidays and all other times. (#1,2,5)

Mile 11.3, Great Bridge Lock-**VHF 13** (3'), **Restricted**: Locking southbound on the half-hour and northbound on the hour. Have bow and stern lines long enough to loop around shore cleats and return to boat. Have registration or document number ready to give to lock master. Plan to tie to north wall. (#5)

Note - For southbound vessels, from mile 11.9 to 188, the wind has more effect on the water height than the tide does. (#5)

Mile 11.9, {0.5}, Great Bridge, (444424), **Free Dock**: Tie up to south wall between lock and bridge. Room for 6-7 boats to tie up. "24 hour limit" is largely ignored. Let bridge tender know when you want to go south. Close to numerous restaurants, fast food, and other shopping. Propane at Exxon station. Watch crossing the road at the bridge. Very heavy traffic. (#5,15)

Mile 12.0, {0.5}, Great Bridge Bridge-**VHF 13** (6'), **Restricted**: Opens on the hour from 6AM to 7PM. Bridge and lock are synchronized. (#5)

Mile 12.1, {0.5}, Great Bridge, (444424), **Free Dock**: Room for 5-6 boats on the dock on the east (southbound) side of the bridge on the north side of the channel. Same shopping applies as mile 11.9. (#5)

Mile 13.9, {0.5}, Norfolk Southern RR Bridge-**VHF 13** (7'): Usually open.

Mile 15.2, {0.5}, Centerville Waterway Marina, (442224): This marina had diesel fuel for $0.70/gal in June 99. (#1)

Mile 15.3, {0.5), Centerville Turnpike Bridge-**VHF 13** (4'), **Restricted**: 6AM to 7PM opens on the hour and half hour only. (#5)

Mile 20.2, {0.5}, North Landing Bridge-**VHF 13** (7'), **Restricted**: From 6AM to 7PM opens on half-hour and hour. Opens only on hour in high winds. (#5)

Mile 28.4, {0.5}, Pungo Ferry Marina, (442224): Transient rate of $0.75/ft + $3.00 electric and diesel fuel for $0.70/gal in June 99. (#1)

Mile 28.5, {0.5}, Pungo Ferry: Two options available: (1) North of old bridge location (344331) you can anchor on the west side in the old river bend in 5' of water. (2) Southwest of the old bridge location (344231) you can anchor in 8-10'. (#15)

Mile 49.5-49.8, {0.5}, Coinjock: Three places for inexpensive fuel:
Mile 49.5, Midway Marina on west bank, diesel $0.65/gal Jun 99. (#1)
Mile 49.6, Coinjock Marina on east bank, diesel $0.65/gal Jun 99. (#1)
Mile 49.6, Harrison's Marina on west bank, diesel $0.65/gal Jun 99. (#1)

Mile 56.5, {0.5}, Buck Island, (333141): Anchor east of "153" close to island in 6-8'.

Mile 57.8, {0.5}, Buck Island, (224141): Anchor SE of Buck in 8.9' close to shore south of where trees are. No protection from south wind. (#5)

Mile 61.2, {0.5}, Broad Creek, (344441): Enter Broad Creek 1.7 miles at 270M degrees from R164. Use caution, some shoaling to port just beyond creek entrance; then stay slightly to north of center to selected anchorage. Anchor in 8-10'. Carried 7' into anchorage in May 97. (#5)

Mile 80.0: Dismal Swamp Canal and Virginia Cut Route junction.

Mile 80-82: **Caution** day markers have been added and existing markers renumbered. Long Point Shoal is marked by new markers. R8 was changed to R10, etc.

Mile 82.1, {0.4}, Little Alligator River, (324341): Go WNW at R10 into Little Alligator River. Favor south shore and stay in 6-10'. Not good in west-northwest wind. (#15)

Mile 84.1, {0.4}, Alligator River Marina: Transient rate $0.70/ft in slip + $3.00 electric and diesel fuel $0.65/gal. Jun 99. (#1)

Mile 84.2, {0.4}, Alligator River Bridge-**VHF 13** (14'): On demand if not windy. Favor east side of channel as shoal is encroaching from west. (#5)

Mile 88, {0.4}, Milltail Creek, (443441): 2 ½ miles east of ICW is a narrow and deep cut through heavy growth. Some love it, and others are nervous about the trees and over hanging branches. We have tied to trees along side the north bank of the Milltail Creek several times and found it to be a wonderful place to tie up in the worst weather.

     From the north, take a course of 127T from ICW marker R16. From the south, take a course of 044T from ICW marker R22.

     Entrance is nearly invisible, but marked with a white post to south of channel followed by another white marker south side on a tree. Stumps are at surface both north and south of this entrance.

     Anchoring in the first 5 miles is very difficult if not impossible due to vegetation on creek bottom. Once to open lake inside, anchoring is no problem. Vessels over 45' will have trouble turning around in the first few miles.

Caution!- In the spring of 96 three boats anchored just off Milltail Creek entrance seeking protection from a strong east Wind. Two of the three boats lost their anchors because they became fouled on old stumps. Anchoring near the shores of the Alligator River can be hazardous to your anchor system or your crew. Use a trip line. Be careful while freeing your anchor.

Mile 101.1, {0.3}, Alligator River, (324241): Anchor south of ICW in 8'+. Lots of space protected from south winds.

Mile 102.2, {0.3}, Alligator River, (334241): Anchor NE of Deep Point in 7-8'.

Mile 103.2, {0.3}, Alligator River, (334241): Anchor south of Bear Point inside R46 in 7-9'. Room for 3-4 boats.

Mile 104.4, {0.3}, Alligator River, (334241): Anchor off Tuckahoe Point in 10'. Use trip line, many snags reported. In strong NE winds, sound your way west to 6' for little better protection. (#15)

Mile 113.9, {0.2}, Fairfield Canal, (244321): Anchor to south of ICW in canal just east of Fairfield Bridge in 5-6'. Well protected from winds and current, but holding is not that good. Some boats tie to trees and shore. Water is deep to shore line.

Mile 114.0, {0.2}, Fairfield Bridge-**VHF 13** (7'), **Restricted**: From April 1 to November 30, 7AM to 7PM, opens on hour and half-hour. On demand rest of the time. New high rise bridge under construction to open 2001. (#1,4,5,12)

Mile 127.5, {0.3}, Pungo River, (334341): North of G23 on Pungo River. Anchor in 7-8'. Not good for south wind. For better protection continue 1.2 nautical miles up river from G23 to large basin at [35 34.00]. Depth to 8' to within 150' of trees on NE shore. Favor SE half of basin as NW third contains shoal. (#5)

Mile 129.5, {0.3}, Scranton Creek, (334441): Follow charted creek 2.5 miles from ICW magenta line first south and then southeast. Stay in center of creek. Anchor in 7-8'.

Mile 131.7, {0.3}, Dowry Creek, (434434): Dowry Creek Marina had a transient rate of $0.75/ft + $3.00 in June 99. (#1)

Mile 135.5, {0.4}, Pantego Creek, (324213): Just off Belhaven anchor in 7-8' near the south shore of Pantego Creek. Be careful of shoal in middle of creek. For better wind and wake protection proceed up Pantego Creek to R12. Take a heading of 290/300M toward fixed bridge. Anchor in 8-10'. Dinghy to NE up canal near G11 on past hospital and tie up near low bridge. (#2,21)

Mile 136.5, {0.4}, Pungo Creek, (334441): Follow channel markers from ICW. Select spot west of G3 depending on wind conditions. Anchor in 7-8'.

Mile 153.7, {0.5}, Eastham Creek, (334241): Follow channel markers from Goose Creek ICW G13 east to between G3 and R4 and anchor just outside the channel in 5-6'. Use trip line on anchor. Can go further up this bight than chart indicates. Fishing boat traffic can rock you morning and night as they go in and out. At least 1 mile to shrimp boat docks with 8' all the way. (#2)

Mile 154.5, {0.5}, Campbell Creek, (324341): West of Long Neck Point, near R14, Campbell Creek offers anchoring about ½ mile in, close to either shore. Lots of crab pots in season. Better protection further up creek if winds pick up.

Mile 157.2, {0.5}, Hobucken Swing Bridge: Removed May 97.

Mile 157.3, {0.5}, RE Mayo Co., (443313): Located on west bank below bridge. Primarily shrimp boat dock. Transient rate $0.20/ft, $0.10/ft for electric. (#1)

Mile 159.7, {0.5}, Gale Creek, (334141): Anchor west of G23 in 7'. Better west of crab pot floats. Use anchor light. (#15)

Mile 160.8, {0.5}, Bear Creek, (334441): Turn west at G27 on Bay River and follow deep water into Bear Creek. Watch shoal just west of G27. Pass it well to the south. Open to winds from east to south.

Mile 173.5, {0.5}, Broad Creek, (334441): Turn north halfway between R4 and R6 on Neuse River and follow markers into Broad Creek. Give Broad Creek "3" a wide berth before heading for R4. Anchor beyond R4 in 7-8'. (#15)

Mile 178.0, {0.5}, South River, (434441): About 3 mi. off ICW, but plenty of places to anchor once past G5. Go a mile or more beyond R6 for delightful solitude and anchor in 10-12'. Several miles of navigable water to explore. Entrance well marked, but red side of channel is shoaling.

Mile 181.5, {0.5}, Oriental: Three options:
  (1) Town dock (444414), **Free Dock,** located at head of bight in town. Turn to starboard at R8 after passing breakwater and proceed to end of bight. Room for 2 or 3 boats drawing 4 ½ feet. "48 hour stay" enforced. Very helpful town to boaters. Town offers grocery, marine store, hardware, PO, etc. (#1,21)
  (2) Anchor in small basin (334313) between fixed bridge and breakwater. New dinghy dock before bridge behind breakwater. (#21)
  (3) Anchor in Greens Creek (334333) in 5 ½ to 6', if you can get less than 45' fixed bridge. Saw only 4' in May 97.

Mile 187.5, {0.5}, Cedar Creek, (334241): Enter either side of Adams Creek G9 and expect as little as 6' near channel. There is limited space with deep water and it can become crowded on weekends. Shrimp and crabs are sometimes available at small commercial dock on creek to right. (#5)

Note - Vessels northbound, wind has more effect on water height from mile 188 to 11.2 than tide.

Mile 195.8, {2.5}, Core Creek, (441114): Bock Marine Builders located just below fixed bridge had a transient rate of $0.75/ft in June 99. (#1)

Mile 202.3, {3.5}, Gallant Cut: **CAUTION:** Gallant Cut into Beaufort, at ICW marker G35, is closed due to shoaling. ICW is **not** closed. Boaters desiring to go to Beaufort coming from the north are advised to use the natural channel starting at "RS" (mile 200.8) and follow it until it intersects Gallant Channel off Gallants Point. Then proceed to Beaufort via the bascule bridge. (#1)

(1) Town Creek, {3.7}, (223213): When entering from between G1 and R2 from Gallant Channel beware of shoal on red side all the way in. Anchor in bight to the north before the marina in 6'+. (#21)

(2) Beaufort Bridge-**VHF 13**(13'), Restricted: From 7:30AM to 7:30PM opens every 20 minutes starting on the hour. This bridge is on the Beaufort channel, not the ICW. (#1,5)

Mile 203.8, {3.7}, ICW RR Bridge: Partially dismantled and inoperative.

Mile 204.0, {3.7}, Beaufort Inlet, Shackleford Banks, (421241): (A little further off the ICW, but offering more space is the Cape Lookout National Seashore area.) Follow the Morehead City Channel towards the Beaufort Inlet. At Shackleford Point turn east and follow the north shore behind Shackleford Banks. Proceed past R2 and anchor in best wind protection. Park maintains picnic area and rest rooms. Wonderful stop for visiting beaches and enjoying anchoring behind barrier island. (#4)

Mile 204.0, {3.7}, Taylor Creek, (321323): Beaufort, NC, with an assortment of stores, provides an excellent stop for the cruiser. The NC Maritime Museum offers a courtesy car to reach more distant grocery stores (2 mi.). Propane at Hills Gas Store, marine parts on Main Street, PO in harbor. Anchor south of channel in front of Beaufort. Very crowded due to popularity. Dinghy dock opposite PO and east of Town Docks. Town Docks will allow you to tie up for 1 hour at no charge to pick up supplies, mail, etc. Beaufort Marine offers free electronic mail service for boaters with a computer and modem. Strong currents, exposed anchorage, and wakes have made some cruisers rate this anchorage as less than favorable. (#4,5,15,26)

Mile 205.0, {3.7}, Morehead City, (431214): Tie up overnight at the Sanitary Restaurant for $10. No electric. Pay at reservation desk. To locate, when southbound, turn to starboard just past the Morehead City Terminals at mile 204.9 and follow the channel behind the unnamed island. Restaurant has green canvas awnings and is located on land on north bank where chart says "Subm Pile".

Mile 205.1, {3.7}, Morehead City, (331213): Anchor in 8' in small basin north of unnamed island and south of tower, marked on chart. Room for 3 or 4 boats. Channel will carry 5 ½ ' from west and 8' from east.

Mile 209.3, {1.5}, Peletier Creek, (443323): Enter Peletier Creek channel opposite ICW G7 and watch for cross current. 4' reported in the channel at low tide. Short way in at junction of 2 creeks there is room for 2 to 3 boats in 6-8' of water. Well protected. You can dinghy up the east branch to near by shopping. Lots of sport fish boats. (#3)

Mile 210.5, {1.4}, Spooner's Creek, (344422): Enter marked channel to north from ICW G9. Watch for crosscurrents when entering channel. Go past marina and anchor in basin near private homes. A dinghy dock at the northwest most point provides access to a shopping mall with Food Lion, Walmart, McDonalds, Radio Shack, Lowes, and movie. (#7)

Mile 225.5, {2.5}, Ennett Point, **Caution:** When northbound, mile marker "225" is frequently mistaken for a green day mark with no board. Do not make this mistake as it is very shallow around "225". The channel lies to the south, closer to the islands. (#26)

Mile 228.4, {2.6}, Swansboro, (431224): Dudleys Marina had a transient rate of $0.75/ft in June 99. (#1)

Mile 229.0, {2.6}, Swansboro, (221112): Southbound, turn north at G47 and enter White Oak River. Proceed past R4 and anchor between R4 and fixed 12' bridge out of the channel. Expect fishing boats and strong currents. The small town offers a general store with fresh fudge, homemade bread, fancy foods and wine as well as a PO.

Note - Swansboro: This is a good point when southbound to check on the status of the Camp LeJeune firing range. Call the Swansboro Coast Guard and ask about the status. Depending on firing, you may wish to hole up in Swansboro instead of the anchorage at mile 233.5.

Mile 233.5, {2.56}, Factory Channel, (344421): Enter new factory channel east of G55 on north side of ICW. 4' shoal at low water at entrance, but easy to "skip" across. Two boats can anchor easily in 7-8'. Sometimes 5 or 6 will anchor bow and stern. Do not try to land at private docks at factory. (#5,15,21)

Mile 235 to 241, {2.6}, Camp LeJeune: The Firing Range can be closed for hours. Normal delay is 1-2 hours. (#18)

Mile 240.7, {3.5}, Onslow Beach Bridge-**VHF 13** (12'), **Restricted**: Opens on hour and half-hour. (#12,21,24)

Mile 244.5, {3.6}, Mile Hammock Bay, (244221): Basin dredged out by military for use with Camp LeJeune. Popular anchorage between Morehead City and Wrightsville Beach. Channel at R66 is shoaling at entrance. Be sure to stay in middle when entering basin. Holding variable, best holding on north side. Let anchor settle in 6-7' and then set. Use anchor light at night due to military maneuvers. Shoreline is restricted military property. (#5)

Mile 246.9, {3.6}, New River Marina has very low diesel fuel prices. $0.59/gal June 99. Transient rate on exposed wall, 9' deep. (431122) $0.50/ft includes electric. (#1,5,15)

Mile 260.7, {3.4}, Surf City Bridge-**VHF 13** (12'), **Restricted**: From 7AM and 7PM only opens on the hour. Stay in channel while waiting for bridge. (#5)

Mile 263.8, {3.5}, Sloop Point, (432331): Turn SE just past ICW marker R86 and before "BC". Stay 50-100' off Port bank and follow marked channel into Topsail Sound. Anchor E of G21 near G19 or ¾ mile further between R14 and G13, north of charted Island and shoal. Do not recommend a draft greater than 5' trying this anchorage. (#15)

Mile 278.1, {3.4}, Figure Eight Island Bridge-**VHF 13** (21'), **Restricted**: From 7AM to 7PM opens on the hour and half-hour. (#4,5)

Mile 283.1, {4.5}, Wrightsville Beach Bridge-**VHF 13** (19'), **Restricted**: From 7AM to 7PM opens on the hour only. (#5)

Mile 283.2, {4.5}, Wrightsville Beach, (331113): Turn SE between markers R24 and G25 and follow channel to beach area. Anchor in dredged area behind Wrightsville Beach beach in 10'. Can get choppy if wind and current oppose each other. New floating dinghy dock is part of "sport fishing" area on SE end of fixed bridge. 2nd dinghy dock opposite split in hotels but only marked on roadside, not visible from water. (#2)

Mile 295.1, {4.5}, Carolina Beach, (334222): Exit ICW to south at marker G161 and follow channel to island in Carolina Beach Basin. Anchor in 15-20' east of G5 between marker and island. Waterfronte Villas and Marina just inside basin on starboard had a transient rate of $10 per night in June 99. (#1,2,4,5,7)

Caution: The loran towers located just north of Snow Cut will cause your loran to become erratic for miles on either side of this point. In addition, TV and radio reception may become goofy. (#1)

Mile 297.1, {4.3}, Carolina Beach State Park, (444421): Enter basin in marked channel between G163 and G165. Channel and basin 4' at low tide. Manager advises that there is only 3' inside at low tide. We went in and found 4' at low water. Tie up for the night with water and electric for $16. (#1)

Mile 297 to 309, {4.6}, **CAUTION**: Channel markers between Snows Cut and Southport have been renumbered. Add 4 to each number on the chart.

Mile 308.6, {4.9}, Bald Head Island Marina, (434322): During the winter season, Nov 1 to Mar 31, this marina charges $.50/ft, 30A $5. Secluded barrier island with virtually no automobile traffic. Marina basin can get real rough due to storm surge in a south to west wind. Bicycles $10/day. Golf cart $30/day.

Mile 309.0, {4.9}, Southport, (444414), Convenience store 1 mile north on Howe street. Past propane fill, auto/marine parts, Italian restaurant, Chinese restaurant, several ATMs, and pizzeria. Post Office 5 blocks NE on E Nash Street. Three stops: (#1)
(1) Turn north into old Southport basin and proceed past fishing docks to starboard to T-pier on port. Tie up to designated "T-Pier". **Free Dock:** Room for 1 boat, no electric, 4' deep at low water with very high pier. Register with police. Limited to 24-hour stay. Water, fresh produce in stand near water tower, and seafood nearby.
(2) The Provision Company in the harbor has one **free dock** also which will hold 2 40' boats. The Provision Company is a low building with green canvas on the north side of the harbor. Free overnight with meal. No electric.
(3) In addition, some boats anchor (444212) in this very limited basin. (#7,13)

Mile 310.2, {4.9}, Dutchman's Creek, (311231): Turn north off ICW past marker G5. Shallower than charts indicate. 4' shoal reported at entrance 1997. Stay close to starboard bank for best water. Narrow, 2 anchors recommended due to strong currents and little wind protection. Lots of bugs. (#15)

Mile 311, {4.9}, Pipeline Canal, (344441): Turn north off ICW after you pass R8 into dredged canal. Caution, submerged dam at 5' low water. Proceed 200 yards and enter basin on port. Favor the east side on entering basin for 6' at entrance to basin. Anchor in 8-10'. Used as hurricane hole by locals. Boat ramp there. Several boats reported having problems finding the deeper water. However, it is there. (#1,4,17,23)

Mile 320.0, {4.9}, Lockwoods Folly Inlet: Shoaling continues to be a problem. Follow the new floating buoys. Never saw less than 10' in May 98. (#1)

Mile 330.5, {5.4}, Shallotte Inlet, CAUTION: Do not follow the sea buoys by mistake. This turn at the inlet is most deceptive when northbound. Follow ICW markers (watch for yellow day marks) closely at this inlet. The red inlet buoy, R12, has been repositioned and is less deceptive now. (#1)

Mile 337.9, {5.4}, Sunset Beach Pontoon Bridge-**VHF 13** (0'), **Restricted:** Opens only on hour. Underwater cable, wait for the bridge tender to signal you through. (#1,19,20,23)

Mile 341.7, {5.4}, Little River, (331132): Turn NW into Calabash Creek before ICW R2, and anchor in 6-8' out of the channel. Significant current and wakes. Take dinghy up Calabash Creek to enjoy many fine seafood restaurants at Calabash. Shoaling reported at R2 in 1999. A short way up Calabash Creek on port is the Marsh Harbour Yacht Club in a protected basin. Their transient rate was $0.75 + $4.00 electric in June 99. (#1)

Mile 344.6, {5.4}, BW's Marina, (431112): BW's Marina on north bank had a transient rate of $0.50/ft; minimum $25. June 99 (#1)

Mile 345.9, {5.4}, North Mrytle Beach: Inside basin at end on west bank, Mrytle Beach Yacht Club had diesel for $0.74/gal. Jun 98 (#1)

Mile 347.0, {5.4}, Anchor Marina, (441224): Anchor Marina had diesel fuel at $0.75/gal in June 99. (#1)

Mile 347.3, {5.5}, Little River Bridge-**VHF 09** (7'): On demand.

Mile 354.3, {3.5}, North Myrtle Beach: New high rise bridge under construction. (#1)

Mile 354.4, {2.2}, Barefoot Landing, (442324), **Free Dock**: 500' floating docks next to outlet mall. Very popular and fills up early. 72 hour limit. No electric or water. Rafting expected. Hang fenders on your outboard side as well. Convenience store across main highway from mall. Many restaurants in mall. Local bus travel to Myrtle Beach shopping. Bus departs 7:30AM, 8:35AM, 10:30AM, 11:50AM, 12:05PM, 1:20PM, 2:30PM, 4:15PM, and 5:30PM. Fare $1.00. (#1,2,4,5,15,19,23)

Mile 370.9, {2.1}, Socastee Bridge-**VHF 09** (11'), **Restricted**: Opens on ¼ and ¾ hour. Still in operation even though new high rise bridge has been built. (#4,12,15,21)

Mile 374.8, {2.4}, Waccamaw River, (342441): Anchor above island and NW of G 25 opposite Enterprise Landing. Can enter ox-bow from either end. Wake from ICW stops at sunset. Trip line a good idea anywhere on Waccamaw River.(#15)

Mile 375.5, {2.4}, Waccamaw River, (442241): Anchor in oxbow at G29 on west side of river. Enter from either end. Use trip line. (#20)

Mile 377.5, {2.4}, Bucksport, (322332): Anchor in 7-10' in old river just north of Bucksport opposite marker G35. Enter from south end only. Do not anchor closer than 50 yards to the deserted island/marina. Cables on the bottom. Excellent Bucksport sausage for sale at marina. (#18)

Mile 380.6 or 382.6, {2.4}, Prince Creek, (343441): Enter Prince Creek from the north at "44" and from the south at G53. Stay in mid channel and select anchorage anywhere along creek in 10-30'. Narrow, may require 2 anchors.

Mile 381.5, {3.2}, Bull Creek, (443241): Enter Bull Creek to NW just below marker R48. Give shoal on upstream side a wide berth. Anchor near mouth in 18-20' or go further up around bend. March to May, fishermen float shad nets down stream in this area.

Mile 388.9, {3.9}, Thoroughfare Creek, (344441): Enter opposite G73 and proceed up stream in 10-12' until you are off 30'+ white yellow sandbank to the east, near charted location of Belin. For real protection go into the mouth of Guendalose Creek and anchor in 10'. (#23)

Mile 396.0, {4.1}, Butler Island, (322241): Enter either north or south of island and anchor near island. Avoid north bank due to shoal. Boat leaving area upstream of shoal hit uncharted underwater object 1995.

Mile 403.0, {4.3}, Georgetown, (233323): Leave ICW opposite R40 and proceed up Sampit River to town north of island. Anchor in area opposite clock tower. Use care in setting anchor. When mill is operating and wind direction is wrong you may get a dirty **residue** on your boat. Town has dinghy dock at small park west of town clock. Town has hardware, restaurants, propane, ice, etc. close to dock. Piggley Wiggly supermarket is about a 1-mile walk, but will pick up and deliver. Pretty much closes up on Sat and Sun. Public library 6 blocks NW has free Internet access. Northbound, if you leave at high tide, you will carry a fair tide all the way to Barefoot Landing. (#1,2,4,5,13,15)

Mile 415.4, {4.6}, Minim Creek, (331431): Turn in to Minim Creek off ICW near marker R4. Go around first bend. Water shallower than indicated on chart, but can accommodate 8' at low water just past large dock. No trees. (#5,15,28)

Mile 420.1, {4.6}, South Santee River, (311331): Leave ICW either left or right and anchor in 8-12'. No trees.

Mile 430.0, {5.8}, McClellanville: Leland Marine Services provides dockage (431214) for 3 to 4 boats at $.60/ft. $2.00 for electric June 99. This is a rough working dock. Proceed up Jeremy Creek to find Leland Marine. (#1)

Mile 430.0, {5.8}, Five Fathom Creek, (321242): Leave ICW at McClellanville and follow Town Creek channel to Five Fathom Creek. Stay clear of marked wreck on the north side at the junction of the first creek. Anchor in any of the creeks just off Five-Fathom Creek and just out of channel. No trees.(#1)

Mile 435.7, {5.8}, Awendon Creek, (311341): Leave ICW at R48 and round point into Awendon Creek. Once past 20-30' water anchor in 7-15'. Open to wind behind bushes. (#4,15)

Mile 439.0, {5.8}, Graham Creek, (311341): Approach creek near marker R64 and proceed south down Graham Creek. 6' at bar at mouth at mid tide. Deeper inside. No trees. (#4)

Mile 448.0, {5.8}, Price Creek, (311341): Approach creek from little north of R86 favoring south bank of creek and stay alert for shoaling at point on that side. Inside creek depths hold almost to bank. Anchor in 8-11'. No trees. (#4)

Mile 451.5, {5.8}, Whiteside Creek, (411441): Enter Whiteside Creek on NW side of ICW, and anchor in 10-12' past deep water. Deep to banks and no trees. (#4,5)

Mile 456.0, {5.8}, Seven Reachs Creek, (421231): Turn SW at G115 and anchor in 7' behind island. Two anchors recommended due to current.

Mile 461.0, {5.8}, Inlet Creek, (211321): Turn north off ICW just west of G119 and enter Inlet Creek. Depths good on north side, not as deep as charted. Don't go beyond first bend, shoaled in. Can be lots of crab traps. A couple of boats reported fouling their anchor on sunken dredging equipment. Use trip line. (#15)

Mile 462.2, {5.9}, Ben Sawyer Bridge-**VHF 09** (31'), **Restricted**: M-F (except holidays) closed 7AM to 9AM and 4PM to 6PM. Holidays and weekends opens only on the hour 9AM to 7PM. On demand all other times. (#2,18)

Mile 464.1, {6.2}, Cooper River: 7 miles up the Cooper River on the port side is the Cooper River Marina, which offers overnight docking with electric for $0.70/ft. The marina office is almost two miles from marina and this marina is isolated.

Mile 469.3, {6.2}, Charleston, (321113): Anchor in Ashley River downstream from City Marina on either side of channel. Dinghy dock at City Marina. Wonderful city to visit. Unfortunate that there is no real good anchorage near by. The Dash buses make touring the city easy; $2 for a day pass. Harris Teeter and Piggly Wiggly supermarkets on bus route. Note that the fixed bridge between the City Marina and Ashley Marina is only 55'. Ashley Marina had diesel fuel for $0.75/gal in June 99. (#1)

Mile 470.8, {6.0}, Wappoo Creek Bridge-**VHF 09** (31'), **Restricted**: (1) From Apr 1 to May 30 and Oct 1 to Nov 30 M-F closed 6AM to 9AM and 4PM to 6:30PM. Opens on the hour and half hour from 9AM to 4PM. Weekends and holidays opens on the hour and half-hour from 9AM to 7PM. (2) From Dec 1 to Mar 30 and Jun 1 to Sep 30 M-F closed 6:30AM to 9AM and 4PM to 6:30PM. Opens on the hour and half hour from 9AM to 4PM. Weekends and holidays opens on the hour and half-hour from 9AM to 7PM. On demand all other times. (#5)

Mile 471.1, {6.0}, Wappoo Creek, (441321): Anchor in 10-12' south of ICW behind island. Enter either east or west of island. Recommend two anchors due to current and large number of boats that use this anchorage. Dinghy to boat ramp on west side north of Wappoo Creek bridge. Walk over bridge and 2 blocks you will find a Piggley Wiggley, Rx, and Chinese Restaurant. (#1)

Mile 476.1, {6.0}, Ross Marine: Floating docks, $.75/ft if space is available. Pay the security man. Electric but, no water. Normally a repair yard, but allows transients if space permits. (#1)

Mile 479.3, {6.5}, Limehouse Bridge-**VHF 09**(12'), **Restricted**: Mar 15 to Jun 15 and Sep 15 to Nov 15, M-F 6:30AM to 9AM and 4PM to 6:30PM opens on hour and half-hour. 9AM to 4PM opens on the hour and every 20 minutes thereafter. On demand rest of the time.

Mile 479.8, (7.0}, Johns Island, (331331): Anchor in ox-bow behind island at mile 480 in 6'. Enter from east end only. (#15)

Mile 488.2, {7.5}, Church Creek, (332441): Turn off ICW at G77 and proceed east into Church Creek about .3 miles. Watch for shoaling on north bank. Anchor slightly closer to south bank. Small stand of trees on south bank. (#5)

Mile 490.1, {7.5}, Yonges Island, (321111): In a NW wind you can anchor in 15-20' above the shipyard off east bank of Yonges Island along side ICW.

Mile 495.4, {7.3}, Toogoodoo Creek, (331341): Enter about ½ mile downstream from R102. Watch for shoal extending down stream as well as shoal on west bank. You can find about 15' if you stay between the center of the creek and the starboard bank. Once inside anchor in 10'. Plenty of room. Proceed upstream 2 miles for even better protection.

Mile 495.7, {7.4}, Tom Point Creek, (432441): Entrance is straightforward NW from ICW. Proceed, favoring port side, about 1.5 miles upstream for wind protection on both sides by trees and anchor in 8-11'. One of the better anchorages in this area. Watch for 8' bar at entrance.

Mile 497.0, {7.3}, Steamboat Creek, (423441): Turn south on North Edisto River at R110 and proceed 1 mile to entrance of Steamboat Creek. Proceed up stream past R2 about a mile and anchor in 17' in front of octagonal building. Boat ramp to land dogs. (#21,23)

Mile 501.5, {7.2}, Fishing Creek, (321441): Turn to NW off ICW at R132. Pick your spot and anchor in 12-18'. Quite buggy. No trees. (#26)

Mile 504.2, {7.3}, South Edisto River, (321441): Upon leaving Watts Cut at G143, turn upstream into south Edisto River. Favor midstream and go around bend and anchor in 7-11'. Trees NE side. (#5)

Mile 505.8, {7.3}, South Edisto River, (422241): Head NW from G149 into charted white water near west shore.

Mile 509.4, {7.3}, South Edisto River, (323141): Anchor NW of G157 near shore or follow shoreline around towards range "C" front marker. Generally protected from NW and W in 10-13'. Watch for shoals indicated, which are generally marked by crab pots. The crab pots also mark the shoreward limits of the anchoring area. Trees on the NW side.

Mile 511.2, {7.2}, St. Pierre Creek, (432341): Proceed down the South Edisto River 3.3 miles to entrance to St. Pierre Creek. Proceed up St. Pierre Creek about 2 miles and select anchorage based on wind direction. Good anchorage, but somewhat off the ICW.

Mile 511.4, {7.2}, Ashepoo River, (321231): Turn downstream from R164 and anchor next to Fenwick Island for wind protection from NE to E. Trees on E bend.

Mile 511.6, {7.2}, Ashepoo River, (321131): Anchor north of ICW between R164 and G165 next to Fenwick Island for protection from N to NE wind. Trees on NE bend.

Mile 513.5, {7.2}, Mosquito Creek: Leave ICW at marker R166 and proceed up Ashepoo River 1.3 miles to Mosquito Creek. Follow creek upstream close to starboard shore. Shoal of 7' at entrance. Two options.
       (1) B&B Seafood (431211) has room for 1 or 2 boats at floating dock. $15 for night. $5 for electric. Fresh shrimp can be purchased at office.
       (2) Or, proceed to first bend in creek and anchor (331211) in 11-13' just beyond B&B Seafood.

Mile 516.1, {7.6}, Rock Creek, (332441): Leave ICW at marker G177 and go north up Rock Creek. Good spot to wait for weather to cross Coosaw River. Favor the east shore to the first bend as you leave ICW. Then, ease to west bank to next bend. Depth drops quickly beyond that point. Lots of bugs at dusk.

Mile 530.4, {8.6}, Brickyard Creek, (434221): Turn off ICW to east between G217 and G219 and anchor where chart shows 11'. Look for shoal of 6' at low water at entrance. Stay in center for best depths. Wakes die down at dark as does flight activity at Navy base nearby. (#4)

Mile 533.4, {8.6}, Beaufort River, **CAUTION: Stay** south of a line between G229 and G229A. Sand bar is shoaling into channel.

Mile 533.8, {8.6}, Beaufort River, (422231): Halfway between G229A and G231 proceed north and west following the shoreline to get behind the shoal at G229 and G229A. Anchor in 10-15' with plenty of room. Less current than Factory Creek or anchorage at Beaufort. (#20)

Mile 534.5, {8.6}, Marsh Harbor Boatyard, (441421): Transient space for $0.60/ft with electric, June 99. Usually full, with little space for transient. Call ahead. (#1)

Mile 535.9, {8.6}, Factory Creek, (331313): Turn off ICW to south just east of Ladies Island Bridge. Follow channel around and select anchorage for best wind protection. Lots of "no see ums". Dinghy to Ladies Island Marina and it is a short walk to good shopping. (#4,5,15)

Mile 535.9, {8.6}, Ladies Island Marina, (431314): Up Factory Creek on starboard, this marina had transient space at $0.75/ft. Jun 99 (#1,18)

Mile 536.0, {8.6}, Ladies Island Bridge-**VHF 09** (30'), **Restricted**: Opens only on hour from 9AM to 4PM. No opening from 7AM to 9AM and 4PM to 6PM. The rest of the time on demand. (#19)

Mile 536.3, {8.6}, Beaufort, (321322): Anchor north of ICW below marina. Beaufort has a lot to offer, interesting museum, restaurants, etc. Lots of "no see ums". Swift current may require two anchors.

Mile 536.3, {7.4}, Beaufort, (421324), **Free Dock**: Tie up to 180' floating day dock at south end of marina. You can stay all day at no charge. No docking from 12 midnight to 6AM. 6' depth at low water alongside. At full flood or ebb, it can be tricky getting in close to the dock, unless you have good control of your vessel. There is also 500' of wall just above the marina where you can tie up for $0.50/ft. However, because of the high tide, swift currents and rough walls, it is not recommended except for a short stop at near high tide and slack water. (#4,5,15)

> **Downtown Marina**
>
> First class marina with floating docks.
> Well stocked ships store.
> Convenient to all facilities in the area.
> Courtesy car!
> Courteous staff.
> **Skipper Bob books**

Mile 538.0, {8.6}, Beaufort Memorial Hospital: BMH has installed a 20' emergency floating dock.

Mile 544.5, {8.6}, Cowen Creek, (431431): Leave ICW near G33 and proceed up Cowen Creek 3.5 miles following the chart. Anchor where creek narrows beyond second bend.

Mile 553.8, {8.0}, Skull Creek, (322231): At Seabrook Lodge, head south parallel to shore about 100' off. Proceed into slot with marina dead ahead, dropping hook in charted 10-11'. Lots of fishing boats, use anchor light. Few trees on SE.

Mile 556.5, {8.2}, Hilton Head Hbr, (421224): Outdoor Resorts Marina had a transient rate of $0.75/ft + $3.00 Elect and Diesel for $0.70/gal in June 99. (#1)

Mile 563.7, {8.7}, Broad Creek, (231122): Leave ICW to SE and round G1 into Broad Creek. Follow Broad Creek for about 3 miles to just above Opossum Point. Anchor near south shore below Palmetto Bay Marina. Good protection, but ferries use this creek. Shelter Cove Marina 6.3 miles up Broad Creek on the starboard side had diesel fuel for $0.75/gal in Jun 99. (#1,15)

Mile 565.5, {8.4}, Bull Creek, (421241): Leave ICW to north before R34 and proceed up Bull Creek. Go past first bend for additional wind protection and more reasonable depth. (Less than 20') Few trees to NE. Lots of small boat traffic.(#12,23)

Mile 568.8, {8.3}, Cooper River, (321431): Leave ICW NW at G37 and proceed up Cooper River 1.5 miles to about opposite higher pair of power poles. Drop hook inside charted 12' contour area, which extends to about middle of river. Lots of wildlife.

Mile 570.1, {8.1}, New River, (421431): Enter New River 2/3 the distance between G39 and R40. Proceed NW up New River staying 100 yards off south bank. Pick your spot before water gets deep at first bend. No wind protection, no trees. (#15)

Mile 572.6, {8.1}, Wright River, (411441): Leave ICW to south at R48 and proceed down Wright River ½ mile. Anchor in center as sides shoal. No trees.

Mile 576.0, {8.8}, Savannah, (421123): To visit this city, leave the ICW where it crosses the Savannah River and go up stream 8 miles to the **free dock** opposite the cotton exchange. Call Susan Garrison, 912-651-6451 to arrange to stay on this dock. No electric. You can tour the waterfront and many of the old homes. (#14)

Mile 577.5, {8.8}, St Augustine Creek, (411441): South of ICW between marker R8 and R10. Proceed up stream ¼ to ½ mile and anchor in 20-25'.

Mile 579.9, {9.2}, Causton Bluff Bridge-**VHF 13** (26'), **Restricted**: M-F, closed 6:30AM to 9AM and 4:30PM to 6:30PM. Opens to pass traffic at 7AM, 8AM, and 5:30PM. On demand at all other times. (#5)

Mile 582.0, {9.2}, Tidewater Boat Works, (441324): Tidewater Boat Works had transient rate of $0.70/ft +$3.00 electric in June 99. (#1)

Mile 584.4, {9.2}, Herb River, (431422): Leave the ICW opposite G37 and favor the Thunderbolt side of the Herb River. Proceed ½ mile upstream and anchor in 13-15'. Upper stretch of river is the local hurricane hole. Can dinghy to Palmer Johnson Marina at Thunderbolt for supplies. (#5,15)

Mile 590.0, {9.1}, Isle of Hope, (331313): Just off the ICW on the west side in the Isle of Hope is a popular anchorage, which may be a problem if your boat has a draft over 4'. Deeper water closest to ICW. Marina charges $5 for dinghy dockage.

Ride is available to Pearl's for dinner or public transportation is available to (#2,4,5,28)

Mile 592.8, {9.1}, Skidaway Narrows Bridge-**VHF 13** (24'): On demand.

Mile 594.8, {9.1}, Moon River, (311231): Enter half way between R74 and G75 and favor south bank. Entrance only 4' at LW, but good anchorage once inside. No trees. (#2)

Mile 606.5, {8.5}, Redbird Creek, (421441): Leave ICW when southbound just before G99 and enter Redbird Creek headed NW. On entering, stay slightly left of mid stream, then ease to right to first bend. Anchor mid stream beyond 2nd bend in 19'. Depths less, but more uniform than shown on chart. Should be able to carry 6' draft into creek at LW. No trees. (#15)

Mile 608.6, {8.5}, Buckhead Creek, (431441): Leave the ICW near marker R102 and head east for about a mile and then follow Buckhead Creek around to the south. Pick your anchorage according to winds in 15-20'. Favor mid channel. For north wind, go in lee of Pine Island. Trees only on Pine Island. Don't go up creek at Pine Island as it is shoaled. Anchoring (431441) in Cane Patch Creek is another option. Anchor in middle past first turn. (#17)

Mile 611.7, {8.8}, Bear River, (411141): Anchor on the north side of the ICW opposite R104C where chart shows 10'. Good depth 50 yards off shore. No trees.

Mile 612.5, {8.8}, Big Tom Creek, (331441): Leave ICW just south of G105 and enter Big Tom Creek mid stream, then favor south bank. Anchor about ¼ mile off ICW or go around bend and pick spot with less than 15' at LW. Use 2 anchors to limit swing. (#15)

Mile 613.9, {8.8}, Kilkenny Creek, (332431): Leave ICW and head NW from G107. Hold to center of Kilkenny Creek (> 12' all the way) or slightly to north side. Anchor up stream 2 miles (off BBA charts) before marina in about 11' near where stream enters Kilkenny Creek from south. Can also anchor in the stream from the south in 17' to avoid some of the wake problems. Also can anchor past marina in front of houses.

Mile 619.0 or 623.5, {8.3}, Walburg Creek, (421431): If southbound leave the ICW at R114 and round "C" to the east. Follow the contour of St. Catherines Island and proceed up Walburg Creek, staying mid stream. Anchor near houses where Walburg Creek turns west. If northbound, leave the ICW at R124 and proceed east. Avoid charted shoals and proceed to bend where Walburg Creek turns north. At half tide, found 9' where chart shows 4'. Anchor near houses. Trees on east side. Buggy. (#18)

Mile 625.5, {8.3}, Cattle Pen Creek, (332441): Enter by heading NE from position about 2/3 distance from G127 to R128. Shoals on both sides of entrance. Go in ¼ to ½ mile staying in center or slightly to east. Further upstream, depth gradually decreases to 6' or less at LW. Second anchor may be needed to limit swing. (#12,15)

Mile 630.0, {8.7}, Wahoo River, (321441): Head up Wahoo River from G135 about 2 miles. Depths hold until upstream of Wahoo Island. Select spot with trees on north shore to provide some wind protection. Other areas all marsh. (#15)

Mile 643.5, {8.4}, Crescent River, (433421): Leave ICW at marker G157 and head west up Crescent River. Stay to mid stream. After 1 mile, turn to port into small creek with island in the center and head for small fishing village. Leave island to your starboard and follow small creek up past shrimp boat docks. Anchor past shrimp boat docks mid stream in 10-12'' LW. Water shoals quickly beyond fishing village, so do not go more than ¼ mile above village. Alternately, anchor (332441) in 12-15' in the Crescent River just past the small island at the next bend. (#1,5)

Mile 644.1, {8.4}, Shellbluff Creek, (431421): Leave ICW just south of R162 and head west just past fishing dock. Anchor in 8'. (#12)

Mile 646.6, {7.8}, New Teakettle Creek, (421441): Leave ICW to north between R172 and G173 and proceed up New Teakettle Creek mid stream. First bend past Mary Creek offers a good choice in 15-20' with lots of room. No trees.

Mile 649.3, {7.8}, Duplin River, (432231): From R178 on Doboy Sound head NE into Duplin River avoiding shallow water on west side. Proceed about 1 mile up river past ferry landing and anchor in 15'. There are trees on the both the east and west bank for wind protection. Landing nearby for pets. (#23)

Mile 651.3, {7.8}, Back River, (421231): Turn east off ICW between G181 and south side of Doboy Island. About half way along south shore, ease south towards crab pots and into area charted at 8-9'. Lots of swinging room, yet well protected. Shrimp boats raft here, so be sure to show anchor light. Trees to north.

Mile 651.6, {8.5}, Darien River, (311441): Turn west off ICW north of R184 and proceed up Darien River mid stream. Anchor in 12-15' with plenty of swinging room. Shrimp boats use the Darien River so use anchor light.

Mile 653.7, {8.5}, South River, (311441): Leave ICW SE from marker R190 and head down South River. Swing wide around points to avoid shoals. Anchor in 10'. Good swinging room. No trees.

Mile 655.5, {8.5}: **Caution:** South bound, past R194, what appears to be R196 is actually a northbound range marker. West side of channel is dry at low water.

Mile 661.9, {8.3}, Two Way Fish Camp, (441432): Two Way Fish Camp up South Altamaha River has transient rate of $0.75/ft in June 99. (#1)

Mile 661.9, {8.0}, Broughton Island, (411441): Head NW from G219 and follow marked channel towards Fridaycap Creek staying about 100' off starboard shore. Bottom shoals sharply from 20' to 6', so pick spot with eye on swinging radius. Easier to enter than chart indicates. Anchor about where chart shows 13'. No trees. Busy so show anchor light. (#5)

Mile 658.0, {8.2}, Altamaha River: Stay 200 yards off R206 and R208. Channel is shoaling from the West.

Mile 665.7 or 667.4, {8.4}, Frederica River, (431431): If southbound, leave ICW just before G229 and turn SE down Frederica River. If northbound, leave ICW just past G241 and turn NE up Frederica River. Only 5' at low water on south entrance to Frederica River. Frederica River is deep and well marked, follow midstream. At bend just south of Fort Frederica, anchor in 11-15' towards western bank. Dinghy dock available to visit Fort at high tide. $2 admission fee. (#15)

Mile 666, {8.4}, Wallys Leg, (421441): Leave ICW west at marker G231 and head up Wallys Leg. Saw 6-9' going upstream and no 30'. Favor southern shore to avoid shoal and anchor near area marked "Wallys Leg" on chart. (#23)

Mile 673.0, {8.2}, Frederica River, (411233): From ICW proceed east past marker G241 down the old ICW channel towards fixed 9' bridge. Anchor in 17'. Dinghy to Golden Isles Marina (see below). (#35)

Mile 677.2, {8.0}, Lanier Island, (211222): From ICW proceed east at marker G249 and head for R2. At R2 turn north on range markers and proceed 1.5 miles up stream near Golden Isles Marina. Anchor south of marina and allow anchor to settle in silt before setting. Marina provides dinghy dock for $5 so you can go shopping and sight seeing on St. Simon Island. (#15,18)

Mile 680.0, {8.0}, Brunswick, (444424): Brunswick Landing in the basin in downtown had transient rate of $0.75/ft and diesel fuel at $0.74/gal in June 99. (#1)

Mile 684.3, {7.7}, Jekyll Island Bridge: Removed May 97. Watch for shallow water west of channel.

Mile 685.9 and 695.6, {7.7}, Little Satilla River: Alternate route to by pass St. Andrew Sound. 5 miles longer, but worth it if St. Andrews Sound is acting up. Shallow in spots. Recommend 6' draft using only on ½ tide or better. To use the alternate route southbound turn west at G25. To use it northbound, turn NW at R40. Favor Red A4 and give Green A5 a wide berth. Anchor (331441) off alternate route by turning west at RA4 and proceed up Umbrella Creek and anchor in 10'. (#2)

Mile 691-696: Watch for wild horses on Cumberland Island.

Mile 695.6, {8.2}, Floyd Creek, (311341): Turn NW off ICW into alternate route on Floyd Creek and anchor inside protection of creek. Use anchor light as this is a designated channel. No trees. (#28)

Mile 696.1 or 703.8, {8.2}, Brickhill River, (433441): When southbound, leave ICW headed south below marker R40 and follow Brickhill River up stream favoring the east bank. Pick your best wind protection in first bend. When northbound, leave ICW headed north at marker R62 and use your chart to avoid marked shoals. Can traverse entire river in 8' or more. Also can anchor near Plum Orchard Dock. Dinghy to dock and walk to north end of Cumberland National Seashore. Lots of alligators. (#12)

Mile 697.5, {8.2}, Shellbine Creek, (422441): Leave ICW headed north from just NE of marker G43 and head up Shellbine Creek. Stay on starboard side entering and anchor according to wind conditions.

Mile 711.0, {7.3}, Drum Point Island, (421231): Leave ICW headed NE from marker R40 and follow eastern shore. Anchor between Dungeness and Greyfield on Cumberland Island. Visit National Seashore area by dinghy. Dinghy dock is 2nd dock you will pass entering anchorage area. Entrance fee $4. Short walk to ocean beach. Very unpleasant if strong north or south wind because of opposing current. (#2,5,15,21)

Mile 712, {6.8}, Lang's Marina, (431212): Leave ICW and head west at marker G35. Follow St. Marys River staying in marked channel 3 miles to Lang's Marina, with floating docks. Just past two large mooring balls on starboard in St. Marys. $.75/ft, + $3.00 electric. Monitors Channel 16. Restaurants in walking distance, but no grocery stores. (#5,10)

Mile 715.8, {7.0}, Florida Petroleum Pier: Diesel fuel is available at Florida Petroleum Pier in quantities of more than 100 gallons. Fast delivery nozzle and new pilings. Diesel fuel $0.73/gal and transient rate $0.75/ft in June 99. (#1)

Note - Several boats have reported that Florida marinas added a "local tax" to the price shown on their pump. In reality, Florida added a sales tax to diesel fuel sold to pleasure craft. The tax was supposed to be added to the pump reading, but since the sales tax is not charged to commercial vessels, some marinas add it after pumping your fuel. You may pay 6-7% more than the pump price at some marinas in Florida. (#1)

Mile 716.5, {7.0}, Fernandina Beach, (411113): Anchor west of ICW between R10 and R12. Use dinghy dock at Fernandina Harbor Marina for free if just coming ashore. $5 if using marina facilities. Reasonable shopping within 5 blocks. May tie up at Fernandina Harbor Marina complimentary for up to 1 hour. 2 to 4 hours is $.20/ft/hr. Grocery store 4 miles. Call them for a ride both ways. Shrimp festival the 1st weekend in May. Big event with booths and good food. (#2)

Mile 719.5, {7.0}, Jackson Creek, (421311): Leave ICW between marker G3 and G5 and head east into Jackson Creek. Anchor in 9'.

Mile 720.8, {7.0}, Kingsley Creek RR Bridge-**VHF 09** (5'): Usually open unless train coming.

Mile 726.0, {6.3}, Alligator Creek, (321431): Leave ICW at marker R36 and head north behind island to anchor near mouth of Alligator Creek. (#15)

Mile 726.5, {5.8}, South Amelia River, (421131): Leave ICW between markers G39 and G41 opposite Harrison Creek. Proceed to eastern shore and work north behind shoal to anchor in 10'.

Mile 735, {5.6}, Ft. George River, (431131): Leave ICW to east, north of G73, and follow markers to G5. Anchor east or west of G5. Trees south side. Dinghy to plantation on Fort George Island or go to Little Talbot Island and walk across to ocean beach. Lots of local traffic (#5,15,23)

Mile 739.1, {5.1}, Sisters Creek Bridge-**VHF 09** (20+4'): On demand. (#5)

CAUTION - Tidal current on the St. Johns River can be as high as 4 knots where the ICW crosses the river. Be sure to watch your side drift while crossing the river **and** watch for large ocean going ships both coming up and down the St. Johns River.

Mile 739.5, {5.1}, Jacksonville: Depart ICW at St. Johns River and proceed up stream 14 miles to visit Jacksonville, FL. It is important that the tidal currents be taken into account at the junction of the ICW and the St. Johns River. Tidal current switches up stream 3 hours after low tide at Mayport.
(1) 16 SM up river just past the Matthews Bridge in Jacksonville, swing around the south end of Exchange Island and anchor (321122) in 8-10'.
(2) 18.5 SM up river downtown river walk provides day docking for shopping.

(3) Beyond the Fuller Warren Bridge the St. Johns River opens into a wide body of water with little current and a small tidal range. A short way further up it becomes fresh water and provides for a great cruise for the next 100 miles with lots to see and very reasonable dockage fees.

Mile 744.2, {4.6}, Pablo Creek, (331331): Leave ICW just south of G17 and proceed behind three islands on east side. Do not try to go between these islands! Anchor in about 20'. Use trip line because of rubble on bottom.

Mile 747.4, {4.8}, Jacksonville Beach: Enter basin on west north of McCormick Bridge and follow well marked channel to day marks 11 and 12. Only 3 ½' in channel at low tide. . Large shopping mall 3 blocks including supermarket and Wal-Mart. Two stops:
   (1) Harbour Lights Restaurant, (444424), **Free Dock**: The last marina in the basin offers overnight accommodations including electric and water at no charge for those guests that eat in the restaurant.
   (2) Jacksonville Yachts, (444424), 1st marina on port had a transient rate of $0.55/ft in June 99. (#1)

Mile 747.5, {5.9}, McCormick Bridge (31+4'), **Restricted**: Apr 1 to May 31 and Oct 1 to Nov 30. M-F 7AM to 9AM and 4:30PM to 6:30PM, opens on hour and half-hour. S-S and Holidays, 12 Noon to 6PM, opens on hour and half-hour. All other times on demand. (#2)

Mile 758.7, {5.6}, Eddie's Restaurant, (442321): 100' north of Palm Valley Bridge on the east bank provides docks. Vessels can stop there at no charge when stopping for meal. Be cautious, sign on dock says "No Water at Low Tide". (#4,5)

Mile 758.8, {5.6}, Palm Valley Bridge-**VHF 09** (9'): On demand.

Mile 765.0, {5.0}, Pine Island, (322441): Leave ICW to east about 100' south of G25. Stay well off south bank of creek. Less water than shown on charts. Anchor in 8-12'. Some distant trees both east and south. Lots of mosquitoes. (#15)

Mile 769.5, {5.0}, Tolomato River, (331131): From ICW marker R42 head northeast and work your way up into pocket behind marker G39. Indian burial mound on shore. Trees to the east.

Mile 773.0, {5.2}, Cap's Seafood, (421121): Tie up at no charge at two floating docks east side of G51 if stopping to eat. Walk to beach. Exposed to winds north to SW. Large wakes from passing traffic.

Mile 773.5, {5.2}, Oscar's Old Florida Grill, (421121): Floating docks on east bank just off R52 made out of two sections out of alignment. No water or electric. Can stop for no charge if eating at grill. Short walk to beach.

Mile 775.8, {5.2}, Vilano Beach Bridge: Removed 1996. (#20)

Mile 776.0, {5.2}, St. Augustine Inlet: **Caution** - Be sure to pass R60 on its ocean side. It is easy to cut this turn short and run aground.

Mile 776.6, {5.3}, Salt Run, (424312): Leave ICW at marker G1 and enter Salt Run channel. Follow markers, and proceed about 2 miles south beyond marina. Anchor just east of marker G7 in 8'. (#15)

First Mate Ships Store

Inside Comachee Cove
Yacht Harbor.
ICW Mile 775.7
Large selection of marine hardware.
Charts and chart kits.
904-824-5605
Skipper Bob books

Mile 777.8, {5.3}, St. Augustine, (321123): Anchor north of Bridge of Lions. Less crowded and less current than anchorage south of bridge. Deep water close to shore. But, more exposed to north through east winds. (#5,15)

NOTE - St. Augustine City dock charges $7 for landing dinghies from noon to noon. Charge includes trash disposal and showers. City has much to see and is important historical spot to visit. PO is handy as well as marine parts store. Do not tie your dinghy to the concrete wall north of marina and restaurant. This wall is dry at low tide.

Mile 777.9, {5.3}, Bridge of Lions Bridge-**VHF 09** (18+2'), **Restricted**: M-F 7AM to 5PM opens on hour and half hour **except does not open** at 8AM, 12 Noon and 5PM. Weekend and holidays 7AM to 6PM opens on hour and half-hour. On demand all other times. (#5,19)

Mile 778.1, {5.3}, St. Augustine, (431123): Just south of Bridge of Lions anchor out of channel to west in 8-10'. Wakes die down at night.

Mile 781.2, {4.0}, Matanzas River, (311131): Leave ICW north of R18 and proceed south into pocket behind shoal. No trees.

Mile 785.2, {3.8}, Matanzas River, (311121): Anchor off ICW just south of marker R38 in pocket of deeper water.

St. Augustine Municipal Marina Ships Store

Marine parts
Snacks
Nautical gifts
Nautical books
Charts and chart kits
Handy to downtown
St. Augustine
Skipper Bob Books

Mile 786.2, {3.5}, Butler Beach, (324421): Leave ICW at G43 and hug east shore as you enter basin behind Butler Beach. Anchor in 6-7'. Not much room. Use two anchors. Trees and houses on east Shore.

Mile 788.7, {3.0}, Crescent Beach Bridge-**VHF 09**(23+2'): On demand.

Mile 792.4, {2.5}, Fort Matanzas, (331121): Leave ICW south of G81 and head down center of Matanzas River. 8' as you leave ICW, anchor in 8-10'. Trees north and south. Must dinghy to park dock on NE shore to get park tour.

Mile 792.5, {2.5}, Matanzas Inlet: **CAUTION:** Waterway shoals towards west in inlet area. Three new green markers between G81 and G83 move channel close to west bank. Southbound **very hard to see** the new markers until almost on them. Deepest water is only 20' off west shore. (#1,15)

Mile 809.1, {1.2}, Cement Plant, (344411): Turn west off ICW between markers G11 and G13 and anchor in dead end channel near abandoned cement plant. Sea Ray plant may wake you starting as early as 6:30AM. Many boats usually stop here. May have to use two anchors to limit swinging. (#23)

Mile 810.5, {1.0}, Flagler Beach Bridge: Removed October 1996. (#20)

Mile 812.9, {1.0}, Flagler Beach, (344331): On west side south of R20 are two underdeveloped canals. They offer good protection for an anchorage with trees on both sides. Variable holding. Enter the southern most of the two canals and favor the south side. 5' at LW. Use two anchors. Some barge activity in north canal. No landing.

Mile 816.0, {0.9}, LB Knox Bridge-**VHF 09** (15'): On demand.

Mile 829.0, {0.7}, Seabreeze, (324113): Small anchorage east of ICW just north of dual Seabreeze Bridge.

Mile 829.1, {0.7}, Seabreeze Bridge removed Sep 97. (#4,21)

Mile 829.2, {0.7}, Seabreeze, (334313): Anchor east of ICW marker R32 in 6-9'. Watch for sunken boat about 250 yards south of bridge and 80 yards east of channel. Only 4.5' of water over this boat.

Mile 829.7, {0.7}, Main Street Bridge-**VHF 09** (18+4'): On demand. New high rise bridge under construction. (#1)

Mile 830.1, {0.9}, Broadway (Carleton Blank)Bridge-**VHF 09** (14+4'): On demand.

Mile 830.6, {1.5}, Memorial Bridge=**VHF 09** (17+4'), **Restricted**: M=S closed 7:45AM to 8:45AM except at 8:15AM and closed 4:45PM to 5:45PM except at 5:15PM. On demand Sunday, holidays and all other times.

Mile 830.7, {1.5}, Memorial Bridge, (333323): Use green marker to north basin of Halifax Harbor as a back range. Turn east and head straight towards shore until 100' off bank. Turn south and anchor. Dinghy across ICW to south basin of Halifax Harbor and tie up at dinghy dock at West Marine at north end of south basin. (#4)

Mile 831.9, {3.4}, Daytona Beach, (323122): Leave ICW to west at marker R44, then come north along shore to anchor in between R40 and R42 in 8=12'. Buoy anchor due to trash on bottom. Check chart for cable area and sewer outfall. Wide open to wind and waves.

Mile 835.2, {4.7}, Seven Seas Marina, (431321): Dockage $0.50/ft, $2 electric. Jun 99. Strong current in channel on entering. No stores near by to speak of, but can walk to beach. Incredible breakfast at on site diner. (#1)

Mile 836.7, {2.7}, Adventure Yacht Harbor, (433324): Located behind spoil islands on east side this marina had a transient rate of $0.75/ft + $3.00 electric June 99. (#1)

Mile 839.5, {2.7}, Upper Ponce de Leon Inlet: **CAUTION:** Four new buoys mark the channel. 2A, 2B, 3A, and 3B. 7' at low tide. Stay between red and green.

Mile 841.7, {2.7}, Power Basin, (344221): Anchor in small basin west of ICW next to large yellow building. Near "stack" on chart. Room for two boats with two anchors.

Mile 842.2, {2.7}, Rockhouse Creek, (421231): Turn NE into Rockhouse Creek between R10 and R12. Anchor in 8=10'. Show anchor light.

Mile 845.0, {2.7}, Coronado (George Munson Memorial) Bridge=**VHF 09** (21+3'): On demand. (#19,20)

Mile 845.2, {2.7}, Coronado, (431224): River View Hotel and Restaurant, on the east bank south of the Coronado Bridge had a transient rate of $0.75/ft in June 99.

Mile 845.4, {2.7}, Sheepshead Cut, (341213): Southbound enter at G33 off ICW and head SW. Anchor in 8=13'. Northbound enter at G41 in marked channel. Don't anchor near west end of island. Bottom badly fouled. Do not anchor too close to north side, as it is shallow. New CG channel markers behind island severely limits anchoring room. Try to anchor south of channel. Dinghy to New Smyrna Beach dock next to bridge. Walking distance to Food Lion, bank, etc. (#4,5,15)

Mile 845.5, {2.7}, Causeway Marine, (444324): North of island and R38. Enter behind island from east end only. Transient rate $0.60/ft with electric. Jun 99. (#1)

Mile 846.2, {2.7}, New Smyrna Beach, (441224), **Free Dock**: Tie up to one of two curved docks north of bridge on west shore. Room for approximately 4 boats. "4 hr limit" sign posted. Vessels arriving late and leaving early have generally not experienced a problem staying overnight. Walk to Food Lion, restaurants, bank, etc. (#5,15)

Mile 847.3, {2.0), New Smyrna Yacht Club, (431122): Leave ICW to west at R46. Members of any yacht club $.50/ft. Transient docks on east side of island and one behind island in much better protection.

Mile 847.8, {2.0}, New Smyrna Beach, (312421): Turn east halfway between G47 and G49 and enter deep water behind small island, where 12' is marked on chart. Favor the south side as the channel follows the south shore. Anchor no more than 30 yards off south shore just clear of ICW. Anchor in 12-14'. (#17)

Mile 861.3, {1.0}, Mosquito Lagoon, (313141): Leave ICW just south of G19 and head 060M to charted area of 7'. Least depth after leaving channel was 6'. Shoal draft vessel can work east almost 1 ½ miles to barrier island.

Mile 862.8, {1.5}, Mosquito Lagoon, (313141): Turn east at marker R24 and sound way east and south, mostly latter, to pocket of deeper water. Locate spot charted as 10', east of submerged pile. Buggy, but a lot of bird and sea life.

Mile 869.1, {0.5}, Haulover Canal Bridge-**VHF 09** (24+3'): On demand, unless closed for space shots. (#5)

Mile 869.5, {0.5}, Haulover Canal, (344331): Just past bridge southbound, turn to port into basin used to launch small fishing boats. Small basin, room for 2 or 3 boats on two anchors. Stay at center on entering basin and anchor in east half of basin in 6'. Small boat traffic abounds during the day, but dies down at night. Manatees swim around your boat day and night. Go slow! (#5)

Mile 876.7, {0.5}, Jay Jay RR Bridge (7'): No radio. Usually open, but closes automatically when train approaches.

Mile 876.8, {0.5}, Jay Jay RR Bridge, (434431): Turn east just south of bridge and run parallel to tracks. Feel your way in and anchor in 7-14'. Good protection from north and NE winds.

Note - Mile 877 to 935, Indian River: The tide has almost no effect on the height of the Indian River because of the large surface area and small inlets. On the other hand, strong prolonged winds raise or lower the water level. Don't anchor in skinny water if strong winds are forecast.

Mile 878.1, {0.3}, Titusville: Titusville offers shopping within walking distance, fast food, PO, etc. Also great tourist spot to arrange for rental car to visit Disney World or Kennedy Space Center. Budget Rent-a-car will pick up at marina. Good bus service to Cocoa, Merritt Island, etc. Call 407-633-1878 for schedule. Westland Marine in Titusville basin had transient rate of $0.75/ft + $5.00 electric in June 99. Two anchorages in Titusville covered below: (#1)

Titusville Municipal Marina
Floating docks
Diesel and Gas
Long term and transient rates
Well-stocked ships store
Convenient to downtown
Rental Car access
Convenient to Orlando and
Cape Kennedy
Skipper Bob Books

Mile 878.2, {0.3}, Titusville, (324123): Anchor west of the ICW and north or south of Titusville Municipal Marina channel in 7-9'. Dinghy to Municipal Marina and use facilities for $5 per day. Food store, propane fill, and Laundromat easy walking distance. (#15)

Mile 878.6, {0.3}, Titusville Bridge-**VHF 09** (9'), **Restricted**: Closed 6:15AM to 7:15AM and 3:15PM to 4:30PM. 15' available in 10' of water in first span east of opening span. On demand rest of time. (#2)

Mile 878.7, {0.3}, Titusville, (324122): South of Titusville Bridge, turn either east or west into charted deep water. Anchor in 15-18' for wind protection from the north. Avoid charted shoals.

Mile 882.2, {0.3}, White Post, (424341): At R38 steer 070M towards white post (Separating spoil banks) Leave post to port. Proceed 1 to 1.8 miles and anchor in 7-8'. Great spot to watch shuttle.

Mile 883.8, {0.3}, Indian River City, (314221): Depart ICW at R40 and head NE sounding way into 7-8'. Good place to watch space launch, but not much else.

Mile 885.0, {0.3}, Addison Point, (324221): Either north or south of Addison Point Bridge, leave the ICW east and sound your way in to protection of causeway in 7-8'. Better spot to watch space launch from. Dinghy to causeway and walk to Astronauts Hall of Fame (look for rocket). (#4)

Mile 885.0, {0.3}, NASA Causeway Bridge-**VHF 09** (23+3'), **Restricted**: M-F closed 6:30AM to 8AM and 3:30PM to 5PM. Also closed during space shots. On demand at all other times. (#2,15,20)

Mile 893.6, {0.3}, Canaveral Barge Canal: Popular spot to enter or leave ICW for ocean. Use chart 11476. Anchor in 6' west of the lock just below spoil island while waiting to go out on ocean, or when returning from the Bahamas. Excellent spot to watch space launch. Heavy local traffic on weekends. If you cross the Barge Canal, you can go south on the Banana River to rejoin the ICW at mile 914.3. Must be able to clear fixed 36' bridges and navigate in 5' of water.

Mile 897.5, {0.3}, Two inexpensive marinas are located just north of the Cocoa Bridge. Both located in basin to the east. Island Point Marina (434324) is $0.60/ft plus $2.50 for 30A electric. Indian Cove Marina (444414) is $0.50/ft plus $1.50 for 30A. Jun 99. Dredged to 4.5'. (#1)

Mile 897.8, {0.3}, Cocoa, (324122), **Free Dock**: Leave ICW south of Cocoa Bridge and proceed west sounding way in between bridge and electric lines. Anchor in 8-9'. 200' of dock (434324) provided for tie up at base of bridge on north Causeway bank. Will carry 5' to dock edge. Shoal west of dock and sign with "No Overnight". Town of Cocoa has hardware, antique, specialty shop, etc. SF Travis and Co., the east coasts best hardware store is 2 blocks west of the dock. Library with Internet access is 6 blocks west and north. (#2)

Mile 898.8, {0.3}, Rockledge, (424223): Leave ICW at G77 and proceed west to anchor in lee of Rockledge in west wind.

Mile 909.0, {0.3}, Palm Shores, (324121): Anchor in protection of causeway either north or south of Palm Shores Bridge depending on wind direction. Proceed east and sound your way in, avoiding charted shoals. Can dinghy ashore on causeway.

Mile 914.2, {0.3}, Indian Harbor Beach, (334323): Also known as "Dragon Point". Proceed east from ICW towards G1 at mouth of Banana River. Stay close (100') to "1" on rounding point. Anchor in 10' in mouth of Banana River near Indian Harbor Beach. Very popular and crowded. For more protection, proceed north through Mathers Bridge about ½ mile and anchor in 8' to west of channel just north of bridge. Mathers Bridge is on demand 6AM to 10PM only. Does not open other times. Can dinghy to Anchorage Marina and tie up for $2 per day. Short walk to grocery, restaurants, etc. (#2,5,15,24)

Mile 914.4, {0.3}, Eau Gallie, (324122): Anchor in protection of causeway either north or south of Eau Gallie Bridge; depending on wind direction. Proceed west and sound your way in, avoiding charted shoals. Can dinghy ashore on causeway.

Mile 914.7, {0.3}, Eau Gallie, (444323): Follow marked channel south of Eau Gallie Bridge NW from R2. Channel will carry 6' all the way in to the protected basin.
(1) Room for 2 boats to anchor north of entrance channel past park. Dinghy to park dock both north and south of channel near entrance.
(2) Eau Gallie Yacht Basin had transient rates of $0.75/ft in June 99. (#17)
(3) Waterline Marina had a transient rate of $0.50/ft in June 99. (#1)

Mile 918.2, {0.3}, Melbourne, (324122): Anchor in protection of causeway either north or south of Melbourne Bridge; depending on wind direction. Proceed east and sound your way in, avoiding charted shoals. Can dinghy ashore on causeway.

Mile 925.3, {0.3}, Rock Point, (314221): Leave ICW just north of R20 and proceed west to clear tip of spoil island. Then turn south and anchor in 8' behind either of the first two islands. Pleasant "fair weather" anchorage. (#15)

Mile 933.9, {0.3}, Sebastian River Marina, (434324): Inexpensive marina behind spoil island by G55. Transient rate $0.50/ft plus $3.50 for 30A. June 99 (#1)

Mile 935 to 877, {0.3), Indian River: The tide has almost no effect on the Indian River because of the large surface area and small inlets. On the other hand, prolonged strong winds tend raise and lower the water level, depending on wind direction.

Meter 937.6, {0.3}, Marinas, (434324): Two inexpensive marinas west of R66. Capt Hiram's Sebastian Marina had a transient rate of $0.60/ft and $3.50 30A. Sembler Marina had a rate of $0.50/ft plus metered electric. June 99. (#1)

Mile 945.7, {0.5}, Jones Fruit Dock, (433121): Tie up at Jones fruit Dock east of marker R104 for $10 per night. Electric by extension cord $3 extra. Great fresh fruit at fruit stand. Use of phone usually permitted. Room for 4-5 boats. (#1)

Mile 946.4, {0.5}, Pine Island, (334231): Depart ICW north at R112. Head directly toward the south tip of the small spoil island south of Pine Island. As you approach the small island ver to the west and anchor close behind the small island and east of Hole In The Wall Island. **CAUTION:** Power cable with 14' clearance NW of this anchorage. (#16)

Mile 950.0, {1.0}, Vero Beach: **Caution,** favor green side of channel near R128. Rock in center at 5.5' known by locals as the "rock pile".

Mile 951.7, {1.0}, Vero Beach Municipal Marina: Anchoring is not permitted in Vero Beach. Leave ICW midway between G139 and the fixed bridge and proceed east following channel to marina. Moorings (431333) $6.42 with 5 day limit. Rafting on mooring balls expected. $1.07 for each person to shower. Check marina via VHF for assignment. Dinghy dock in small cove just north of marina docks.

Marina will hold mail. Supermarkets, drugstores, and restaurants about ¾ mile dinghy ride to fifth canal across ICW below bridge. Two blocks to 2 large malls. Free bus service from marina to all major shopping areas. (#5,15,21,24)

Mile 960.0, {1.5}, Blue Hole, (334431): Head east from ICW north of G171 and follow charted 5' depths and private markers. Turn south off small powerboat marina to anchor off golf course. Found 5' on way in and 8' near shore.

Mile 964.7, {2.5}, Fort Pierce North Bridge-**VHF 09**(21+3): On demand.

Mile 965.5, {2.5}, Port Petroleum Basin, (343223): Proceed west from R186 and anchor in 20' in basin at the west end of Fort Pierce inlet. (#7,34)

Mile 965.6, {2.5}, Port Petroleum Gulf Station: Located at west end of Fort Pierce entrance channel. VHF Channel 10. Diesel fuel $0.72/gal Jun 99. (#1)

Mile 966.2, {2.5}, Causeway Island, (424122): Turn east off ICW north of R188 and follow channel south of Causeway Island. R2 on spoil island. G3 shares sign with manatee warning. R4, G5, G7, G9 and R10 missing as of Nov 97. Anchor (334322) east of R4s charted location and south of channel in 15-20'. Faber Cove, (444422) room for 6-8 boats in 8-10'. Feel your way in, channel is shoaling in 1999. 96 hour limit. (#18)

Mile 973.9, {2.5}, Big Mud Creek, (344421): Turn east off ICW at Mud Creek G1. Follow 4' channel 1.4 miles and anchor in protected basin in 10' next to power plant. Lots of manatees.

Mile 981.4, {1.3}, Jensen Beach, (224121): Anchor in protection of causeway either north or south of Jensen Beach Bridge, depending on wind direction. Proceed west and sound your way in avoiding charted shoals. Can dinghy ashore on causeway. Several blocks to shops and restaurants. (#4,15)

Mile 981.4, {1.3}, Jensen Beach Bridge-**VHF 09** (19+3'), **Restricted**: May 1st to Nov 30th, M-F opens on hour/half hour. On demand rest of the time.

Mile 981.8, {1.3}, Jensen Beach, (424323): South of R220 turn west towards yellow building of marina. Proceed WNW and anchor north of R220 in protection of Causeway in 6-7'. Also inexpensive marina. Anchor's Aweigh Marina had a transient rate of $0.75/ft in June 99. (#1)

Mile 984.9, {1.3}, Indian River Bridge-**VHF 09** (25+3'), **Restricted**: Dec 1 to May 1 M-F 7AM to 6PM opens on hour and half-hour. Rest of the time on demand. (#20)

Mile 987.9, {1.1}, Manatee Pocket, (234312): Leave ICW at St. Lucie Inlet and follow
St. Lucie River channel west to marker R6A. Then follow marked Manatee
Pocket channel south and favor south side after the last pair of markers. Then
cross to the center around the first bend. Anchor in 5-6' between Mariner Cay
and Pirate Cove Marinas and beyond Pirate Cove. Three day limit. Four marinas
in pocket and within walking distance to many stores including West Marine.
Crowded. 6' at low tide. (#17,24)

Mile 987.9, {1,1}, St. Lucie River: Depart for points west via the Okeechobee Waterway.
See subsequent pages in this book starting on page 74.

Mile 992.2, {1.5}, Peck Lake, (234141): Leave ICW south of marker G19 and head
060M. Watch for shoal south of sign. You should find 10' all the way to shore.
Fair weather anchorage. Short dinghy ride to shore and ocean beach is just a
short walk away. Very popular on weekends.

Mile 995.9, {1.8}, Hobe Sound Bridge-**VHF 09** (20+4'): On demand.

Mile 999 to 1001, {2.0}, Hobe Sound, (434121): Anchor short way off ICW in several
deep-water areas. Between R38 and R40 to west, between R40 and G41 to west,
SW of R42, east or west of R44, and west of G49. Go toward shore as far as draft
permits.

Mile 1004.1, {2.1}, 707 Bridge-**VHF 09** (19+4'), **Restricted**: M-F 7AM to 9AM and
4PM to 6PM opens every 15 minutes starting on the hour. Other times on
demand. (#4)

Mile 1004.8, {2.5}, Jupiter Federal Highway Bridge-**VHF 09** (21+4'): On demand. (#20)

Mile 1006.0, {2.6}, Indiantown Road Bridge-**VHF 09** (35'), **Restricted**: 7AM to 6PM,
opens every 20 minutes starting on the hour. On demand all other times. (#4,21)

Mile 1006.1, {2.6}, Indiantown Road Bridge, (344323): Anchor to east in loop. Carries
5' at MLW. Enter and exit at north end near bridge. Land dinghy in woods on SE
end of bridge. Shopping center, movies, groceries, etc. 1 block east of landing.
(#2)

Mile 1009.2, {2.8}, Donald Ross Bridge-**VHF 09** (35'), **Restricted**: M-F 7AM to 9AM
and 4PM to 6PM opens every 15 minutes starting on the hour. On demand other
times. (#1,2,20,21,23)

Mile 1012.0, {3.2}, PGA Bridge-**VHF 09** (21'), **Restricted**: 1 May to 31 Oct, M-F 7AM
to 9AM and 4PM to 5PM opens at quarter past and quarter to hour. On demand
M-F at other times except from 1 Nov to 30 Apr when from 9AM to 4PM opens

every 20 minutes starting on the hour. Weekends and holidays from 8AM to 6PM opens every 20 minutes starting on the hour. On demand the rest of weekends and holidays. (#20)

Mile 1012.5, {3.2}, North Palm Beach, (344421): From ICW head SW into north Palm Beach Waterway and proceed back to second cul de sac on west side. Anchor in 6' in front of private homes. Room for 2 or 3 boats.

Mile 1013.5, {3.4}, Parker Bridge-**VHF 09** (20+4'), **Restricted**: M-F 7AM to 9AM and 4PM to 5PM opens every 30 minutes starting on the hour. On demand M-F at other times except from 1 Nov to 30 Apr when from 9AM to 4PM opens every 20 minutes starting on the hour. Weekends and holidays from 8AM to 6PM opens every 20 minutes starting on the hour. On demand the rest of weekends and holidays.

Mile 1014.2, {3.4}, Lake Worth, (334123): Leave ICW and head east at marker G27. Follow channel to North Lake Worth anchorage. Pick your spot in 9' in the NE corner. Dinghy to landing at north end of lake and lock it to posts provided. Lots of shopping close by including Publix and Eckerds in mall. West Marine north of mall 0.7 miles.

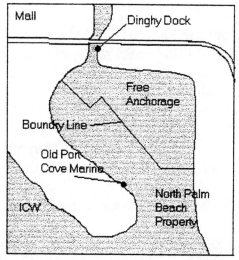

In 1998 the town of North Palm Beach enacted Ordinance No 12-98 which imposes a fee for anchoring in the north end of Lake Worth. If anchored within North Palm Beach property boundaries (see map) the first day is free. After that you must purchase an anchoring permit for 5 days (including the first day) for $30. A police patrol boat will approach you and ask you to decide on the first day whether you will stay beyond 1 day. East of a line between 12 Oaks Marina and R10 is free since it does not lie in North Palm Beach waters. However, this is subject to change as the east side of Lake Worth is also looking at passing the same ordinance as North Palm Beach.

Why did this happen? In 1998 approximately 150 boats decided to stay at Lake Worth because they could not get a good window to cross to the Bahamas. (El Nino) Unfortunately a few of these boaters decided to become a problem. They overloaded private trash cans. One boater checked into a local marina, got a key to the rest room and made copies. Then he passed these copies out to his friends. Late at night they would go into the marina and use the shower facilities without paying. In addition, some of these boats anchored close to Old Port Cove

Marina and made it nearly impossible for those paying for slips to enter and exit the marina. When asked to move these boaters responded with crude language and gestures. Finally, most of the boats at anchor dumped their holding tanks directly into the waters of Lake Worth. In short a few bad boaters have made a mess for the rest of us. The town of North Palm Beach has responded in the only manner they know how. If boat owners won't behave in a responsible manner, the town will make it too expensive for us to stay in their area. Other communities in the same area are looking at the North Palm Beach ordinance and may implement one just like it in the near future. (#1)

Mile 1018.4, {3.3}, Lake Worth, (321121): Leave ICW and head east out Lake Worth Inlet. Just as you approach land on the south side turn south into marked channel, keeping red on starboard. Anchor in 8' just south and west of R6 between cable areas shown on chart. Good jump off point for the Bahamas.

Mile 1021.8, {3.1}, Flagler Memorial Bridge-**VHF 09** (18'), **Restricted**: Nov 1 to May 31 M-F closed 8AM to 9:30AM except at 8:30AM and closed 4PM to 5:45PM except at 4:45PM. From 9:30AM to 4PM opens on the hour and half hour. On demand rest of the time.

Mile 1022.7, {3.1}, Royal Park Bridge-**VHF 09** (14'), **Restricted**: Nov 1 to May 31 M-F closed 8AM to 9:30AM except at 8:45AM and closed 3:30PM to 5:45PM except at 4:15PM and 5PM. From 9:30AM to 3:30PM opens on the quarter to and quarter after the hour. On demand rest of the time including weekends and holidays.

Mile 1024.7, {3.0}, Southern Blvd. Bridge-**VHF 09** (14'), **Restricted**: Nov 1 to May 31 M-F closed 7:30AM to 9AM except at 8:15AM and closed 4:30PM to 6:30PM except at 5:30PM. On demand all other times including weekends and holidays.

Mile 1028.9, {3.0}, Lake Ave. Bridge-**VHF 09** (35'): On demand.

Mile 1031.0, {3.0}, Lantana Bridge-**VHF 09** (12'), **Restricted**: Dec 1 to Apr 30 M-F 7AM to 6PM opens every 15 minutes starting on the hour. Weekend/holiday 10AM to 6PM opens every 15 minutes starting on the hour. On demand all other times.

Mile 1031.1, {3.0}, Lantana, (333123): Proceed west of ICW just south of Lantana Bridge. Sound your way in to bight and anchor in 6-8'. Boats staying over 18 hours must get a permit for $30. Police will come along side eventually to collect money. Stay limited to maximum of 96 hours in any 30-day period. Dinghy to park and lock to sea wall or go to floating dinghy dock at restaurant where food is good and they have "early bird specials". Stores, PO, ice within 4-6 blocks.

Mile 1035.0, {3.0}, Ocean Ave. Bridge-**VHF 09** (10'): On demand.

Mile 1035.9, {3.0}, 15th Avenue Bridge-**VHF 09** (25'): On demand.

Mile 1038.7, {3.0}, George Bush (8th Street) Bridge-**VHF 09** (9'), **Restricted**: Nov 1 to May 31 Weekends and Holidays 11AM to 6PM opens every 15 minutes starting on the hour. On demand all other times.

Mile 1039.6 {3.0}, Atlantic Ave. Bridge-**VHF 09** (12'), **Restricted**: Nov 1 to May 31 M-F 10AM to 6PM, opens on the hour and half-hour. On demand all other times.

Mile 1041.0, {3.0}, Linton Blvd. Bridge-**VHF 09** (27'): On demand.

Mile 1042.1, {2.9}, Pelican Harbor, (244321): Turn west from ICW into man made circular lake. Entrance only 5 ½ feet at LW. Anchor in 6-8'. Set anchors carefully, as some boats have had trouble getting them to hold here. (#23)

Mile 1044.9, {2.9}, Spanish River Road Bridge-**VHF 09** (25'): On demand.

Mile 1047.5, {2.9}, Palmetto Park Bridge-**VHF 09** (19'): On demand.

Mile 1047.8, {2.7}, Lake Boca Raton, (443122): Leave ICW and turn east just north of G65 and run close to shoreline. Anchor in NW corner in 8'. Large shoal in center of lake and 4' or less reported at LW. Can dinghy ashore at ramp on west side of ICW, but cannot leave dinghy. Shopping within one mile. (#12)

Note - Southbound. A lot of bridges, many restricted between here and Miami. You may choose to run this stretch outside. If going down the ICW anyway, try to do so on weekday.

Mile 1048.2, {2.7}, Camino Real Bridge-**VHF 09** (10'), **Restricted**: 7AM to 6PM opens every 15 minutes starting on the hour.

Mile 1050, {2.8}, Deerfield (SR810) Bridge-**VHF 09** (21'), **Restricted**: Oct 1 to May 31 M-T 7AM to 6PM opens every 20 minutes starting on the hour. Fri, Sat, Sun, and Hol opens on hour and half-hour. On demand all other times. (#4)

Mile 1055.0, {3.0}, NE 14th St. Bridge-**VHF 09** (15'), **Restricted**: 7AM to 6PM opens at quarter past and quarter to hour. On demand all other times. (#20)

Mile 1056.3, {3.0}, Atlantic Blvd. Bridge-**VHF 09** (15'), **Restricted**: 7AM to 6PM opens on the hour and half-hour. On demand the rest of the time.

Mile 1056.7, {3.0}, Holiday Inn, (444424): The Holiday Inn Marina had transient rates of $0.75/ft in June 99. (#1)

Mile 1056.8, {3.0}, Lake Santa Barbara, (334221): Turn west into Lake Santa Barbara 1/3 of the way south between marker R74 and R76. Lots of small boat traffic going slow. Anchor in 5-6'. One boater reported being asked to leave as anchoring is no longer permitted in Lake Santa Barbara.

Mile 1056.9, {3.1} Lettuce Lake, (333121): Turn east into Lettuce Lake 2/3 the way south between markers R74 and R76. Anchor in 8-12'.

Mile 1059.0, {3.2}, Commercial Blvd. Bridge-**VHF 09** (15'), **Restricted**: Nov 1 to May 15 M-F 8AM to 6PM opens every 15 minutes starting on the hour. Weekends and holidays 8AM to 6PM opens every 20 minutes starting on the hour. On demand the rest of the time.

Mile 1060.6, {3.2}, Oakland Park Bridge-**VHF 09** (21'), **Restricted**: Nov 15 to May 15 M-F 7AM to 2200 opens every 20 minutes starting on the hour. Weekends/holidays 10AM to 2200 opens every 15 minutes starting on the hour. On demand at all other times.

Mile 1062.6, {3.2}, Sunrise Bridge-**VHF 09** (24'), **Restricted**: Nov 15 to May 15 10AM to 6PM opens every 15 minutes starting on the hour. On demand other times.

Mile 1063.9, {3.1}, Lauderdale Municipal Marina: East side of ICW, $.64/ft. 10 moorings on west side of ICW at $15 per night. Limited to 30-day stay. Always crowded. Can anchor 24 hours near marina where space permits. More marinas up New River. (#1,4,23)

Mile 1064.0, {3.2}, Las Olas Blvd. Bridge-**VHF 09** (31'): On demand.

Mile 1064.5, {3.1}, Lake Sylvia, (334321): Leave ICW headed south at marker R12. Hug the east shore for 6 ½' depth into lake. Once in lake, alter course WSW to avoid a shallow area and anchor in 8-9' where space permits. Police enforce a 24-hour anchoring limit. (#5)

Mile 1066.0, {3.1}, 17th St. Bridge-**VHF 09** (25'), **Restricted**: 7AM to 7PM opens on the hour and half-hour. On demand all other times.

Mile 1069.4, {2.8}, Dania Beach Bridge-**VHF 09** (22'): On demand.

Mile 1070.8, {2.8}, Sheridan St. Bridge-**VHF 09** (22'): On demand.

Mile 1072, {2.5}, Hollywood Marina: In basin on east side of ICW. $0.70/ft. Short bus ride to mall and shopping. Walk across ICW to movies, beach, and convenience store.

Mile 1072.3, {2.5}, Hollywood Blvd. Bridge-**VHF 09** (25'), **Restricted**: Nov 15 to May 15, 10AM to 6PM opens on hour and half-hour. May 16 to Nov 14 weekends and holidays 9AM to 7PM opens on hour and half-hour. On demand all other times.

Mile 1074.0, {2.5}, Hallandale Beach Blvd. Bridge-**VHF 09** (22'), **Restricted**: 7:15AM to 8:15AM opens at quarter after and quarter to the hour. On demand otherwise.

Mile 1077.0, {2.2}, Maule Lake, (344321): Leave ICW and head west from marker R54 through canal with 8' draft. Anchor in Maule Lake in 8-10'.

Mile 1078.0, {2.2}, Sunny Isles Bridge-**VHF 09** (31'), **Restricted**: 7AM to 6PM opens at quarter past and quarter to hour. On demand otherwise. (#2,21)

Mile 1081.4, {2.4}, Broad Causeway Bridge-**VHF 09** (16'), **Restricted**: 8AM to 6PM opens at quarter to and quarter past the hour.

Mile 1079.7, {2.4}, Bakers Haulover Inlet, (422341): North of R6A turn NW, 300M, past Park Point. Anchor in 8-12'. Next to Florida University and day use park.

Mile 1080.3, {2.4}, **Caution:** The ICW is reported badly shoaled between G7 and G9. Depth reported at low tide is 3'. Vessels can go around this problem by following the shoreline near G11 towards the inlet. Once at the inlet, head north following the shoreline until you again intersect the ICW.

Mile 1084.5, {2.4}, Pelican Harbor Marina, (434324): Inexpensive marina in Miami area. Proceed east off ICW in marked channel along bulkhead just before the 79th Street Bridge. Follow the "Red Right Return" rule to the marina. Turn in to marina and dock yourself. No showers, but water and electric. Bus transportation to local shops. Dockage rates recently reduced. Good weekly and monthly rates. They offer a Boat US discount. Miami Yacht allows the use of their facilities for $5 per day. (#4,20,21,27)

Mile 1084.6, {2.4}, 79th Street Bridge-**VHF 09** (25'): On demand.

Mile 1087.3, {2.4}, Julia Tuttle Bridge has a fixed clearance of only 56'!

Mile 1088.4, {2.6}, Miami Beach, (323122): Southbound, leave ICW east just before Venetian Bridge and follow deep water in area of multiple islands. Sound your way in and select the best anchorage for wind protection. Wakes die down at night. Can dinghy up Collins Canal several blocks to Publix, Walgreens and liquor stores.

Mile 1088.5, {2.6}, Venetian Causeway Bridge. Gone June 98.

Mile 1088.7, {2.6}, MacArthur Causeway Bridge. Gone June 98.

Intracoastal Waterway, Miami to Key West

The character of the Intracoastal Waterway changes dramatically at Miami. The water becomes cleaner, the sand whiter and the travel more exposed. Anchorages are harder to find and prudent skippers must plan their day with the weather in mind. The Florida Keys have coral heads under water, most notably on the ocean side of the Keys. Follow your charts closely. Boaters generally arrive at Miami with one of two plans on their minds. (1) Wait for the weather and cross to the Bahamas. Or, (2) move SW and then west and find a place in the Keys to spend the winter.

Boaters going to the Bahamas will only be interested in the first few anchorages listed in this section. For those going down the Keys further, you should already have the BBA Chart Kit, Florida east coast, including the Keys, Region 7, recommended on page 28 of this book. You should get the Cruising Guide to the Florida Keys, 7th edition, by Capt. Frank Papy. Cruisers should note that the Florida Keys bend away to the west after leaving Miami and cruising past Key Largo is almost due west instead of south.

Vessels can follow either of two routes to Key West. Inside via the Intracoastal Waterway for vessels not requiring more than 4 ½ feet of water. Or, outside via the Hawk Channel for all others. Since there are very few anchorages on the Hawk Channel route, all anchorages in this section will be referenced to mile markers on the Intracoastal Waterway and chart name, where available.

At Vaca Key, Marathon, boats may choose to (1) continue on the north side of the Keys in the more protected Intracoastal Waterway, (2) enter the Hawk Channel on the south side of the Keys and proceed on to Key West, or (3) proceed north out of the Intracoastal Waterway and go directly to the west side of Florida.

Boats traveling between Miami and Key West must be aware that there are few spots along the way, where you can safely take a sail boat between the inside and outside routes. It can be done at mile 1098 (Biscayne Channel), mile 1121 (Anglefish Creek), mile 1167 (Channel Five), and mile 1195 (Moser Channel).

Mile 1089.8, {2.5}, Fisher Island, (421221): Leave the ICW just north of G57 and head NE into channel behind Dodge and Lummus Islands. At the end of Lummus Island, bear SE past G5 and follow the deep water to a point south of Fisher Island. Anchor in 10-15' for best wind protection. Some boats use this place to wait to jump off to the Bahamas, but it is not recommended since it is so exposed.

Mile 1091.7 {2.4}, Marine Stadium, (334122): Leave ICW just north of Rickenbacher Bridge and turn east to run parallel to bridge. Proceed towards Rusty Pelican Restaurant. Leave sign to starboard and drop hook in Marine Stadium west of grandstand in 5-7'. Busy, bumpy and noisy on weekend afternoons.

Mile 1092.0, {2.5}, Virginia Key, (323221): Leave ICW and head east at marker G69. Anchor south of Virginia Key in 7' for protection from NW to NE winds. Use anchor light at night.

Note - The "Anchor Police" have arrived. Vessels are now routinely charged $10 plus tax to anchor in any of the four spots listed below. Enforcement seems to depend on how late you arrive and how early you leave.

Mile 1094.0, {2.4}, Crandon Park Marina, (444311): Leave ICW channel north of marker G73 and follow the channel NE towards Bear Cut. Just before fixed bridge, turn starboard into Crandon Park Marina. Dockage $0.70/ft with water and electric Jan 97. Much needed renovation under way. Music can be very loud until 10PM. Within walking distance of Virginia Key and Planet Ocean. Anchoring in Crandon Park Marina basin not allowed. 60 moorings are available at $8 per night. The bus to Miami stops at the marina. (#4)

Mile 1095.0, {2.4}, Key Biscayne, (424221): Leave ICW near MM 1095 and head due east towards G3. Head into small cove to the east located just south of marina. Plenty of swinging room. Not as protected as the two spots below. (#34)

Mile 1095.0, {2.4}, Hurricane Harbor, (334321): Leave ICW near MM 1095 and proceed east towards marked entrance to Hurricane Harbor. While going east keep shoal marker at [25 41.40|80 11.00] on starboard. Watch for R2 to NE and keep it on port. Favor port side going in and anchor inside where room permits. Expect a lot of company waiting to cross to the Bahamas to be anchored here. (#5)

Mile 1096.0, {2.4}, No Name Harbor, (444431): Leave ICW at about MM 1096 and head east for marker R4. Pass R4 and R2 to port and hug southwest shore of Key Biscayne. Follow shoreline around until narrow entrance is visible. Enter harbor and anchor where you can find room. No Name Harbor is another favorite anchorage for those going to the Bahamas. Can dinghy ashore and walk around park. Park closes at night, so be back on your boat before dusk.

Mile 1105.0, {1.9}, Boca Chita Key, (444441): Leave ICW at mile marker 1105 and head SE towards G1 and R2. From the R2 at the end of Featherbed Bank, take a course of about 110M toward shore well south of lighthouse. About half way, you will see six red and green floating buoys leading into well-protected Key Hole Harbor. About 1000' of new bulkhead finished wall tie ups are available. Can carry 5.5' at low water. Toilet, grills, open pavilion, nature trail, etc. Overnight $15, no water. All trash must be carried out. Check bulletin board for reservations. Rangers are present on daily basis. M-F very quiet.

Mile 1112.0, {1.7}, Elliott Key, (423231): Turn east from ICW and approach Elliott Key as close as draft will permit. Protected NE to S. Biscayne National Park on Elliott Key has small boat marina, showers, picnic tables and grills, visitor center, and nature trail. No charges. Park entrance midway up key at R2.

Mile 1120.0, {1.0}, Long Arsenicker, (433241): For wind protection from SW to NE, leave ICW 200 yards south of marker G15 and head west. Be cautious of charted spoil area, SW and right of marked channel. Sound your way in as close under south side of Long Arsenicker as draft permits. Bird nesting area, so need Park Rangers permission to go ashore.

Mile 1120.5, {1.4}, Angelfish Creek, (441241): Leave ICW at about mile 1120.5 and head east across Card Sound to marker R14 on Angelfish Creek. Follow channel through Angelfish Creek and anchor in one of the side creeks. One of the places people wait to cross to the Bahamas. Used by locals as a hurricane hole.

Mile 1121.0, {0.7}, Card Sound, (323241): Head SE from ICW to anchor in the protection of Pumpkin Key in 10'. Avoid rock on north side. Anchor close to key for best wind/wave protection. Deep close to shore of Key Largo SSE from here.

Mile 1128.0, {0.5}, Barnes Sound, (234241): For protection for N to E winds, leave ICW at G27 and head SE and then turn NE and sound your way in to lee of Key Largo, near Steamboat Creek.

Mile 1134.0, {0.5}, Jewfish Creek Bridge-**VHF 09** (11'), **Restricted**: Thursday to Sun and Holiday 10AM to sunset opens on the hour and half-hour. On demand rest of the time.

Mile 1134.2, {0.5}, Blackwater Sound, (433112): South of Jewfish Creek Drawbridge, anchor across the channel from Gilbert's Marina just south of the Anchorage Resort and Yacht Club. There is room for four boats up to 35 feet in water 6-8'. Good protection from northerly winds.

Mile 1140.0, {0.5}, Tarpon Basin, (234233): Anchor either north or south of R48A where chart shows pockets of deeper water. Can get crowded in bad weather. Dinghy dock available at Quay Restaurant, north of and adjacent to Howard Johnson. Tower near HJ helps locate it. About ½ mile south to KMart, TCBY, Publix, Library, etc. North to hardware. Easy walk to Pennekamp State Park ($1.50 admission). Nature movies, boardwalk trail through mangroves and reef trips.

Mile 1143.0, {0.4}, Buttonwood Sound, (234223): Depart ICW midway between marker R54 and G55 and proceed SE. Sound your way in towards shore as far as draft will allow, but not into grassy area. Can dinghy ashore to small basin just north of Yellow building and Snook Restaurant. Do not tie dinghy up at restaurant dock as dinghies have been untied and let loose there. Can also land dinghies well north of yacht club behind opening in mangroves marked with white cone so as to tie up at end of "Dead End" Street. Shopping about 3 blocks.

Mile 1145.0 Hawk Channel, {2.6}, Rodriquez Key, (424221): One of the few anchorages on the Hawk Channel. One of the jump off points for the Bahamas. Anchor north of Rodriquez Key in 6-8'.

Mile 1150.0, {0.5}, Community Harbor, (443323): At R64A turn to R4 and G3 and follow the private channel into harbor. Channel and anchorage 4-5'. (#15)

Mile 1159.8, {0.5}, Cotton Key, (424241): Good protection for N to SE winds. Leave ICW near R84 and head SE and then NE to sound your way as close to Cotton Key as draft will allow.

Mile 1160.0, {0.5}, Islamorada, (424222): For protection from NE to SE winds and shopping. Leave ICW just past R84 and proceed ESE towards shore. Sound your way as close as draft permits. Can dinghy to restaurant dock. Good place to wait for favorable tide at Steamboat Channel. 4-5' at LW.

Mile 1164.0, {0.9}, Lignumvitae Key, (424241): State Park with very interesting tour (10AM, 1PM, and 2:30PM). Anchor NW or E side of Key as close as draft permits. Dinghy to dock to explore Key. $1 per person.

Mile 1167.0, {1.0}, Matecumbe Bight, (424222): For protection from NE to S winds leave ICW at mile marker 1167 and head ESE towards shore. Sound your way in to 6' near shore and anchor. Launch ramp now marked "no trespassing", but may be able to land dinghy at park (woods) ½ mile to west.

Mile 1167.5, {1.7}, Channel Five: Major cross over point for boats going from the inside Intracoastal Waterway route to Hawk Channel or on to Cape Sable and the west coast of Florida.

Mile 1167.5, {1.8}, Long Key Bight, (334231): For protection from winds from the S through W to N leave ICW at mile 1167.5 and proceed SW through Channel Five to beyond fixed bridge. Then turn west and sound your way into Long Key Bight as far as draft allows. Convenient to both Hawk Channel and Florida Bay.

Mile 1195, {2.0}, Boot Key Harbor, (444313): The objective of many boats heading south for the winter. Also known as Marathon. From Hawk Channel enter via Sister Creek with draft of less than 5'. All deep draft vessels enter from west of Boot Key via Boot Key Channel and anchor in area marked "Boot Key Harbor" on chart in 7-8'. Very crowded, with sometimes as many as 200+ boats here. 5 Marinas serve this harbor. (#15)

> Can tie up dinghy at Pat & Kelley's Marina on north side of harbor for $2.50/day or $12.50/week. Access to restaurants and PO about 1 mile. (#1,5)

Dinghy to east end of harbor, about 1 mi. up narrow channel, and tie up at dead end. Short walk to Publix, West Marine, Radio Shack, Scotty's, Ace Hardware, etc.

The rag tag atmosphere and sorry condition of some of the boats in Boot Key Harbor has turned some cruisers off using this harbor in the future. (#5,21)

Mile 1215.0 Hawk Channel, {1.5}, Newfound Harbor, (434223): Best protected anchorage between Marathon and Key West. Do not try to go directly from Hawk Channel R50 to Newfound Harbor Channel R2. That would take you over a couple of coral heads. Stay in Hawk Channel on ICW magenta line until south of R2, then head north to R2 at entrance to Newfound Harbor Channel. Keep R2 about 200' to starboard (shoaling to less than 6' at marker), then favor starboard side of channel past Little Palm Island Resort. From R4, head towards G5 and then R8. Do not head towards R6. From R8 proceed north and sound your way in as far as draft allows. Can carry 4' within ¼ mile of bridge. Dinghy landing on Big Pine Key at east end of bridge. Lots of shopping within 1-mile walk.

Mile 1236.0, {1.2}, Stock Island, (334312): From Hawk Channel, proceed NE into Boca Chica Channel. Follow Boca Chica Channel to marker R8 and then turn NW up Stock Island Channel following G1B to G5B. After G5B, turn to port and anchor in 7'. Dinghy to Maxwell Marine beyond ramp and lock dinghy. Maxwell's has ship's store and block ice. Across road for bus to Key West. (#5)

Mile 1243.0, {1.6}, Key West: The southernmost destination for many boaters. There are a number of marinas, but all are fairly expensive; as is fuel and supplies. Three popular anchorages are available as follows:

Anchor in 10-12' SE of Wisteria Island (332112), or anchor in 8-9' NW of Wisteria Island (324212), or anchor in bight in 10-11' on west side of Fleming Key; NE of G29 (334232). (#15)

From anchorage you can dinghy to Turtle Kraal Restaurant in Key West bight ($2/day or $35/mo), obtain water and dispose of trash. Easy access to Old Town Key West and all the tourist attractions.

None of the above anchorages is really comfortable, and anchoring is not allowed in Garrison bight via long route around end of Fleming Key.

Dry Tortugas

Some 70 miles west of Key West. Lots of sea birds. No water or fuel available and all waste must be removed as you leave. Anchor off the dock at Fort Jefferson on Garden Key and dinghy to nearby beach. Good snorkeling west of fort. Satellite telephone available at fort for $15 per minute. Note that the NE Channel coming into Garden Key filled in to 2-4 feet during a recent hurricane and no longer has the 32 feet shown on most charts. Must go north and then west of Key. Helpful Park Rangers will talk you in if you call them on VHF. (#25)

Okeechobee Waterway

This section covers the waterway between the St. Lucie River at Stuart on the east coast of Florida and the Caloosahatchee River and Ft. Myers on the west coast of Florida, including Lake Okeechobee. The Okeechobee Waterway is made up of the Caloosahatchee River and St. Lucie Canal joining Lake Okeechobee. It is characterized by quiet, serene waterways with abundant wildlife away from the glitzy, fast paced, high cost of living found on either Florida coast.

Before proceeding, get the proper charts. I recommend the BBA Chart Kit, Florida west coast and the Keys, Region 8. Then check with the Corps of Engineers in Clewiston (813-983-8101) for the status of the locks. Each year, the Corps of Engineers closes one or more of these locks for a specific period for maintenance; usually during the summer.

The controlling height is the 49' raised railroad bridge just before the Mayaca Lock. For those with taller masts, you can be unstepped at Stuart or Indiantown, and then restepped at Owl Creek Marina or Fort Myers. Up to a 55' mast can pass by leaning the boat with barrels. See Indiantown Marina for instructions. (#2)

The controlling depth varies, and with lower level changes, can be as little as 5'. Check with the Corps of Engineers if you are in doubt. There is usually little current in either outlet to Lake Okeechobee. However, when Lake Okeechobee is at flood stage (greater than 18') currents on the St. Lucie Canal and Caloosahatchee River can reach 2-3 knots.

Locks on the OWW work on channel 13. The proper whistle signal to request lockage is two long followed by two short blasts. Locks provide lines to secure your boat. The locks of the Okeechobee Waterway are different from all other locks in North America in that they do not use valves to let water in to the lock. Instead, the front gates on the high side of the canal are opened about a foot and the water pours into the lock. In actuality it is not much worse than locks with valves, however it can be a little disconcerting the first time you experience this. Rest assured, they lock pleasure craft through the locks on a regular basis without harm to vessel or crew. **Caution:** Snakes live in the wooden bulkheads in some of the locks. Be on watch. (#20)

Points of interest are referenced to statute mile marker on charts as well as chart name, where possible.

Mile 3.4, {1.1}, St. Lucie River Bridge-**VHF 09** (17+3'), **Restricted**: Dec 1 to May 1 M-F 7AM to 6PM opens on the hour and half-hour. Weekends and holidays 8AM to 6PM opens every 20 minutes starting on the hour. Opens on demand rest of the time. (#22)

Mile 4 to 6, {1.1}, St. Lucie River, (323121): From ICW seek best wind protection by heading E to N from marker G21 and sound your way in as close to shore as draft allows.

Mile 7.4, {1.2}, FEC RR Bridge-**VHF 09** (7'): Usually open unless train is coming (#22).

Mile 7.4, {1.2}, Roosevelt Bridge-**VHF 09** (14'): Does not open if railroad bridge adjacent to it is closed. Opens on demand otherwise. (#22)

Mile 7.6, {1.2}, North Fork, (323221): Leave ICW to north just west of Roosevelt Bridge and follow channel up north Fork a short distance. Turn in to either east or west shore depending on wind direction and sound your way in as far as draft allows. Quieter than St. Lucie River anchorages.

Mile 7.7, {1.2}, Compass Rose Marina, (433324): This marina had a transient rate of $0.50/ft in June 99. (#1)

Mile 7.9, {1.2}, Stuart: Crowded spot popular to replenish supplies.
    (1) You can anchor (323123) off Frazier Creek in 9-10' just east of G23A.
    (2) **Free Dock,** you can tie up (423124) to city dock east of G23A for 4 hours, if space is available. Water available at dock. (#2)
    (3) You can carry 6' into basin and tie to wall from 6AM to 12 Midnight. Frazier Creek entrance is ½ way between G23A and Roosevelt Bridge. Take dinghy up Frazier Creek to a lovely park with cleats along sea wall and small marina for ice. Phones and trash barrels at park. Large grocery store (Publix), and Laundromat about 5 blocks away. (#5,15)

Mile 8.3, {1.2}, Pendarvis Cove, (323122): For NW winds, leave ICW at G25 and head SW. Sound your way toward shore as far as draft allows. Longer dinghy trip to town.

Mile 15, {1.1}, St. Lucie Lock-**VHF 13** (15'): Have fenders on south side of boat for locking. (#1,35)

Mile 15.1, {0.0}, Above St. Lucie Lock: Two options available. (1) Anchor across from campground (344331). Use two anchors to control swing. (2) Tie up at slips provided (444331) at campground for $16. ($8 for Golden Age Passport holders) Slips are short and shallow close to shore. Can get water and dispose of trash at campground.

Mile 28.2, {0.0}, Indiantown RR Bridge-**VHF 09** (6'): On demand except from 10PM to 6AM requires three-hour notice.

Mile 29.4, {0.0}, Indiantown Marina, (444322): 7' depth in basin except at west end. Dockage $.60/ft plus $3 for 30A. Diesel fuel $0.90/gal in June 99. Has 25T lift and is popular place to store boats during summer. $2.50/ft/mo on land and $3.50/ft/mo on concrete. Town is about a mile away. Courtesy car. Saturday evening the owners sponsor an all you-can-eat BBQ. Bring a dish to share. (#2,5)

Mile 36.5, {0.0}, Port Mayaca, (344231): Enter indentation on north side of canal just west of overhead power lines. Anchor in 9-10' with two anchors. Room for 2 boats. Lots of alligators. Buggy. (#15)

Mile 36.6, {0.0}, Port Mayaca, (444441): Enter canal on north side of OWW at [80 34.986]. Dam overflow canal will carry 7' for 200 yards. Anchor where room permits. Room for 2 boats.

Mile 38.0, {0.0}, Port Mayaca RR Lift Bridge-**VHF 09** (6'): Usually open unless train is coming. Make sure it is all the way open if you need 48'. May also be less with high water levels. (#9,18)

Mile 38.1, {0.0}, Port Mayaca, (344221): Anchor on north side of OWW just west of RR bridge where ditch enters canal, but before orange barrels. Sound your way in and anchor bow and stern where draft permits. (#5)

Mile 38.7, {0.0}, Port Mayaca, (444221): Just east of Port Mayaca fixed bridge, tie to dolphins on north side in 6-7'. (#5)

Mile 39.0, {0.0}, Port Mayaca, (324321): Anchor south of lock entrance in large basin. Sound your way in as only 5' is promised. Lots of alligators. (#35)

Mile 39.1, {0.0}, Port Mayaca Lock-**VHF 13** (1'): Put fenders on south side of boat.(#22)

Mile 40.0, {0.0}, Lake Okeechobee: Decision must be made here to go across the lake or take the rim route. The rim route is more scenic but longer (10 mi.). The lake route is shorter, but can get nasty in strong winds. Since there are no anchorages on the lake route, this guide will simply continue with the rim route.

Mile 40 to 44, Rim Route: The Rim Route is twisty and subject to shoaling between markers R2 and R6. A good alternative to this route is to proceed on the lake route to marker G5 and then turn to a course of 170T and head for rim route markers R24 and G25 (4 miles) at [26 54.884|80 36.995]. Least depth seen was 11' in 1998. Can re-enter rim route anywhere between R24 and R34. (#5)

Mile 50.7, {0.0}, Pahokee Harbor, (444422): Manmade harbor on SE rim. Dockage $0.55/ft June 99. Depth 5 ½ to 6'. Can accommodate 50' boat. (#5)

Mile 59.8, {0.0}, Torry Island, (444231): Enter pocket of water west of OWW at [26 42.940|80 42.513] just north of bridge. Anchor in 8' in basin shown on charts. (#5)

Mile 60.7, {0.0}, Point Chosen (Torry Island) Bridge-**VHF 09** (11'), **Restricted**: Opens on demand Mon to Thurs 7AM to 6PM and Fri to Sun 7AM to 7PM. Closed all other times. Uses VHF 09 but slow to respond. Also opened manually and slow to operate. (#22)

Mile 60.8, {0.0}, Slim's Fish Camp Marina, (444211): West of OWW just south of Point Chosen Bridge. $15 overnight & usually full. Camp has few basic supplies. (#1)

Mile 60.8, {0.0}, Town Dock, (444324), **Free Dock:** Just south of Point Chosen Bridge and beside Slim's Fish Camp there is a free dock with 8' alongside. Proceed south past fish camp and swing west toward 200' long wooden dock immediately adjacent to fish camp. 15A electric at fish cleaning stand.

Mile 63.0, {0.0}, South Bay, (334441): Leave OWW just west of launch ramp at 26 41.09|80 44.21 head north into kidney shaped basin shown on chart in blue. 8'+ at entrance and 10-25' in basin. Room for 10+ boats. Lots of birds and alligators. Take dinghy to boat ramp. Walk over hill to pay phone at South Bay Campground. (#22)

Mile 65.0, Lake route (75 Rim route), {0.0}, Clewiston: There is a lock (1') at Clewiston which leads to a marina. No VHF radio. There are no anchorages in Clewiston and no stores other than the marina and restaurant.

Mile 65.2, {0.0}, Clewiston, (444221): Tie up to dolphins north side of OWW just west of Clewiston lock.

Mile 78.0, {0.0}, Moore Haven, (334232): Where the waterway turns SW into Moore Haven, proceed straight ahead into old canal. Stay clear of marina and anchor just beyond fish camp. Best depths on SW bank.

Mile 78.3, {0.0}, Moore Haven Lock-**VHF 13**: Put fenders on north side of boat. Large spaced timbers on lock walls, so fenders do not work well. Be prepared to fend off. (#5,22)

Mile 78.4, {0.0}, Moore Haven RR Bridge-**VHF 09** (5'), On demand except closed 10PM to 6AM. Operated by hand and very slow. (#20,22)

Mile 78.4, {0.0}, US 27 Bridge-**VHF 09** (23'), On demand except 10PM to 6AM opens on 3 hour notice. New high rise bridge under construction June 99. (#20,22)

Mile 78.5, {0.0}, Moore Haven, (444324): City dock on north side provides along side tie up for $0.75/ft, with water and electric. Few small stores available within walking distance. (#1)

Mile 78.6, {0.0}, Moore Haven, (444324): Thomas Dock, just west of city dock on the north side of OWW can take 6 boats for $0.50/ft with water and electric. Tie up and go to hotel across the street t pay. No VHF radio. (#19)

Mile 88.5, {0.0}, Hendry Isles Resort Marina: Room for 5-7 boats to tie up for $12/night with water and electric. 7' depth alongside, but stay in center of channel on entering for best depth. Showers, swimming pool and Laundromat. Courtesy golf cart sometimes available to go to Pinkies. (#1)

Mile 89.0, {0.0}, Glades Boat Storage: Large facility on south bank where boats can be placed in dry storage for $2.50/ft/mo. Usually full. Do-it-yourself maintenance. Sailboats can be stored with mast up. 941-983-3040. Courtesy golf cart sometimes available to go to Pinkies

Mile 92.5, {0.0}, Canal, (444441): Enter canal on north side of OWW at [26 47.577|81 17.25] east of large white building. This canal is referred to by locals as the lollipop. Proceed north in 6' as far as desired and anchor. This is an old quarry canal without much traffic. Deep pool at north end where even larger vessels can turn around.

Mile 93.8, {0.0}, Ortona Lock-**VHF 13**: Put fenders on north side of boat unless otherwise instructed by lock tender. Can tie to dolphins east or west of lock on north side of channel (444321). (#5,19,22)

Mile 94.1, {0.0}, SCL RR Bridge: Removed.

Mile 100.9, {0.0}, LaBelle, (344231): Just east of Port LaBelle Marina at 26 46.42|81 23.30 enter small basin on south side of WW and anchor in 5-8'. Enter on left side of entrance as there is a shoal on right side. Basin shows up as a little pip on the chart east of LaBelle. Manatees and alligators live there. LaBelle Marina was preparing to expand into this basin in June 99 and add 150 slips. Anchoring in here in the future may not be possible. (#1,22)

Mile 101.0, {0.0}, Port LaBelle Marina, (444421): Transient dockage $0.60/ft in June 99.

Mile 102.9, {0.0}, LaBelle Bridge-**VHF 09** (26'): On demand except 10PM to 6AM opens on 3 hours notice. (#19,22)

Mile 103.0, {0.0}, LaBelle: Four spots to stay:
  (1) **Free Dock**: (444324) South side of OWW city dock (3-day stay) with room for three 30-40' boats. 15A electric and water. Short walk to town and good shopping. Supermarket, used book store, Laundromat, restaurants, hardware, bank, etc. (#15)
  (2) On north side of OWW, River Edge Motel and Marina (443222) has 150' of dockage for $.25/ft. (#1)
  (3) 200 yards west on the north side of the OWW (443221) is a boat launch ramp with room for 2 boats to tie up overnight on the face dock.
  (4) Room to anchor (242223) in river if docks are full, but depth is 15-20' and soft mud. (#5)

Mile 108.2, {0.0}, Fort DeNaud Bridge-**VHF 09** (9'): On demand except 10PM to 6AM opens only on 3-hour notice. Slow to respond. Tender must walk from tender house on shore to bridge to open it. (#22)

Mile 116.5, {0.0}, Alva Bridge-**VHF 09** (23'): On demand except 10PM to 6AM opens only on 3-hour notice. (#22)

Mile 119.5, {0.0}, Hickey Creek, (244441): South side of WW anchor behind small island in 7'. Bottom soft mud and poor holding.

Mile 120.2, {0.0}, Franklin Lock: Just before lock westbound, enter basin north of lock. Two choices:
  (1) Corps of Engineers has eight slips (444431) available for $16/night ($8 for Golden Age Passport holders) with water and electric. 5' draft and 40' long maximum.
  (2) Anchor (344431) in 6-10' and dinghy to Corps of Engineer Launch Ramp. Trash disposal and water available. (#5)

Mile 120.4, {0.0}, Franklin Lock-**VHF 13** (2'): Opens 6AM to 9:30PM. Put fenders on south side for smooth lock walls.

Mile 120.5, {1.5}, Franklin Lock, (344431): Just west of lock enter basin on north side in old channel and anchor in 5-10'.

Mile 124.3, {1.7}, Ox Bow, (343433): Leave ICW west of Ox Bow at mile 124.3 and head SE into loop. Anchor in 6-8' for best protection. Dinghy to Jack's Marina and walk to large shopping center 1 mile away with Winn-Dixie. Trees all around and small community on west side of entrance. (#22)

Mile 126, {1.9}, Owl Creek Marina: Do-it-yourself yard or place to store boat during hurricane season (wet or dry storage).

Mile 126.3, {1.9}, Wison Pigott Bridge-**VHF 09** (27'), On demand except 10PM to 6AM opens on three hour notice.

Mile 128.3, {1.9}, Power Plant Slough, (433331): Turn north at G13 and follow white water as charted behind island. Shoal 4-5' at entrance. Anchor 2-300 yards past sign. Found 6' at MLW 50 yards from shore. (#18)

Mile 129.8, {1.9}, Beautiful Island Railroad Bridge-**VHF 09**: Usually open unless train coming. (#22)

Mile 133.8, {1.9}, Ft. Myers Yacht and Shipbuilding: Turn south between R38 and R40 follow row of cement piles to basin. Can step mast here.

Mile 135.6, {2.7}, Ft. Myers, (323121): Turn north off WW at R52 and anchor in charted white water in 5-8'. Avoid marked channel into Hancock Creek.

Mile 146.9, {2.9}, Glover Bight, (334322): Turn northwest off WW before R92 and follow 6' channel NW to Glover Bight. Stay off R2, R4 and R6 in channel due to shoaling to starboard in the channel. After rounding point, and at entrance to marina, go east as far as draft permits. Beware of steep shelving from 15' to less than 5' toward island forming south shore of bight. OK except in SW winds. Most stores 2+ miles away.

Mile 155.2, {2.9}, Deep Lagoon Boat Club, (434334): Had diesel fuel for $0.84/gal in June 99. (#1)

Fort Myers to the Keys via the West Coast

The trip from Fort Myers to the Florida Keys via the west coast is characterized by short trips in exposed shallow Gulf Coast water broken by stops in protected very laid back communities. The wise cruiser will have the necessary charts on board before venturing into this area. I recommend the BBA Chart Kit, Florida west coast and the Keys, Region 8.

For ease of reference, in addition to the chart name of the area, all areas detailed in this section are referenced in statute miles from the Sanibel Causeway Bridge leaving San Carlos Bay near Fort Myers to Marathon in the Florida Keys and calculated by the most protected route a vessel with a 4 ½' draft could prudently take. Miles spent exploring inland areas are not included. In addition, the latitude and longitude will be shown **at the outer mark** for each channel leading to the area described.

It is easiest to think of the trip from Fort Myers to Marathon as a counter clockwise sweep around the southern tip of Florida 145 miles long. While exposed to the west and southwest to the Gulf of Mexico, most of the trip is in shallow water of about

10' and the longest stretch where you must travel outside of protected waterways is only 37 miles.

Remember that the tides on the Gulf of Mexico can be peculiar. They may be diurnal or semi-diurnal, depending on location and/or lunar cycle. Some places have both. See tide tables to be sure. (#9,25)

Mile 0, {2.4}, Sanibel Bridge-**VHF 16** (26'), [26 29.00|82 00.90], **Restricted**: 11AM to 6PM opens every 15 minutes starting on the hour. 10PM to 6AM, opens with 5 minutes notice. All other times opens on demand. (#25)

Mile 1, {2.4}, Pt Ybel, (421231): For an early morning start south, anchor NE of Pt Ybel in 20'. This is a fair weather anchorage.

Mile 3, {2.4}, Estero Island, [26 27.60|81 58.50], (331223): Entering Matanza Pass (8'), follow the marked channel behind Estero Island. After passing under fixed bridge swing to port and follow the channel to the back anchorage. Expect a lot of boats. Can dinghy to good shopping at end of canal south of anchorage. Canal has mangroves to left and house to right as you enter. Free tram runs along beach to take you to KMart, groceries, and laundry. Palm Grove Marina on the north side of anchorage will also allow dinghies to land. (#5)

Mile 4.6, {2.7}, Compass Rose Marina, (444424): This marina had a transient rate of $0.50/ft in June 99. Entrance is tricky. Call on radio. (#1)

Mile 27, {2.8}, Naples, [26 10.40|81 49.00], (343221): Enter Doctors Pass and follow channel to Outer Moorings Bay. Entrance tends to shoal. Dredged 9/96. Carries 7' to R16. North of R16 some 5', go slow. No facilities, but pretty homes. (#25)

Mile 32, {2.9}, Naples, [26 05.50|81 48.70]: Enter Gordon Pass and choose between two anchorages. First, (323321) when you enter you can anchor in Champney Bay (3rd cove to port) near R12. Stay close to west shore when entering. Or second, (322322) proceed up the channel to the north to Naples and anchor near city dock at "35". Space is limited, so look carefully south of channel for a spot and use two anchors to limit swing. 10 free mooring balls are provided south of the marina. Dinghy to the south side of the City Dock and tie up to floating dinghy dock. Market and PO a long walk. Limited shopping close by and some restaurants. Ships store and 2 full service marinas. (#5,15,25)

Mile 32 to 43, {2.6}, Naples to Marco: For boats drawing 4 ½' or less, the old ICW between Naples and Marco makes an interesting trip. Very busy on weekends and strong currents. At high tide a vessel drawing 5' 3" passed through without a problem. Shoaling near G19 and "R8A. Anchor east of G47 in white water (331241) and dinghy west to Keewadin Island and take path to Gulf of Mexico beach. Deserted, lots of shells, and plenty of mosquitoes along the path. At G35 enter the cut behind Little Marco Island and favor the west shore. Anchor in 7-12'. Wonderful solitude! Again you can dinghy to beach. (#21,25)

Mile 43, {2.6}, Marco Island, [25 58.50|81 46.50]: A number of anchorages are available to the cruiser who comes this way. As you enter Capri Pass follow markers carefully as the channel shifts with storms. To starboard on entering proceed behind Coconut Island and anchor in 6-10' (421141). Further inland, just before G15, anchor NW of the marker in 10-12' (331122). Finally, in Factory Bay south of the channel at G15, you can anchor (233322) in the designated anchorage in 6-8'. Holding varies. Be sure to follow the channel into anchorage and do not try to cut across spoil area. Dinghy ashore for limited shopping. Beware of submerged pile roughly half way between G5 and R6. (#25)

Mile 43 to 52, {2.6}, Inside Route: Boats of 4 ½ ' draft can take the inside route from Marco to Coon Pass, via Goodland. A vessel drawing 5' 3" made it at high tide. Travel on a rising tide. Note particularly the change in channel markers at the Marco River Bridge. Red moves to the port side and green switches to starboard. From R2 in Coon Pass, lay course to leave Coon Key Light about 200 yards to starboard. Then approximately 140T to deeper (7-9') water. (#25)

Mile 52, {4.2}, Goodland, [25 55.20|81 39.00}, (443441): Turn west at R6 at Coon Key Pass to Blue Hill Creek. Go past marina on starboard to end of white water for a pretty, well protected cove with good holding. New marina further west with many sailboats, fuel, and some boating supplies. Good place to stop to wait for higher tide or calmer weather outside. (#25)

Mile 63, {2.9}, Everglades City, [25 48.00|81 28.10], (421442): An interesting side trip. Enter Indian Key Pass and proceed up river using the well-marked channel. Turn to NW just before G7 and proceed into Russel Pass. Sound your way in and select best anchorage for wind conditions. If you are up to a visit to Everglades City, proceed on up channel, but be aware of strong currents (up to 2 knots) and shoaling. Shoaling reported between G11 and G11A. Favor SE side of channel between R10 and R12. May be able to tie up in Everglades City for a short time to visit or pay to stay at the Rod & Gun Club, which sells diesel during the winter months only. Also can take dinghy ride to city, but have a good motor. (#5,25)

Mile 100, {4.5}, Little Shark River, [25 18.90|81 08.40], (431241): Enter Little Shark River at marked channel and proceed to R4. For the adventurous, you can follow the Little Shark River to Tarpon Bay or follow the channel to Whitewater Bay. Did find spot at 4 ½ ' LW, but otherwise deeper. Wildlife abounds and good fishing. Mosquitoes active at dawn and dusk. (Bring a shotgun) (#21,25)

Mile 120, {3.8}, Flamingo, [25 05.50|81 05.00], (444431): From the outer marker R2, follow the well-marked channel east nearly 10 miles to the protected basin at Flamingo. Frequent shoaling at entrance channel, proceed slowly. The Everglades National Park Marina provides dockage at $.45/ft without power and $.65/ft with power. Visit the Visitor Center and museum. Small rental boats available as well as bicycles and guided tours.

Mile 120 to 145: Follow the charts and proceed from Flamingo light to Marathon on Vaca Key 25 miles away over 8-10' of water. Reminds you of traveling on the Grand Bahama Bank. Rejoin east coast ICW at mile 1167.5. See page 72.

Fort Myers to Tampa

The Intracoastal Waterway from Fort Myers to Tampa is a protected passage behind barrier islands with clean water, white sand and wild life; broken by over developed communities. One can enter or leave the Waterway at Boca Grande, Venice and Longboat Key. The Sarasota passes require considerable caution. The prudent boater should have the up-to-date charts before beginning this trip. I recommend the BBA Chart Kit, Florida West Coast and the Keys, Region 8.

All places listed in this section are referenced to the ICW mileage shown on the charts, starting at mile 0 on the east side of San Carlos Bay near Fort Myers and ending at Mile 141 north of Clearwater. In addition, the local chart names are used whenever available.

Remember that the tides on the Gulf of Mexico can be peculiar. They may be diurnal or semi-diurnal, depending on location and/or lunar cycle. Some places have both. See tide tables to be sure. (#9,25)

Mile 4.0, {2.4}, St. James City, (322122): Leave ICW just west of R12 and proceed north as close to city as draft will allow. Can dinghy into town for restaurant, but not much else in the way of shopping. (#25)

Mile 5.3, {2.4}, JN Ding Darling National Wildlife Refuge, (333341): When northbound, turn south between R14 and R16. When southbound, turn south between R18 and R16. Feel your way into within 200 yards of refuge shoreline marked by small buoys. Take dinghy into Tarpon Bay and ride rented bikes on trails. (#22)

Mile 8.3, {2.4}, Chino Island, (323141): From ICW proceed north from R24 and anchor south of Chino Island in 7-8'. (#25)

Mile 13, {2.1}, Captiva Island, (344441): From ICW proceed WSW from half way between G37 and R38 towards marked channel into Roosevelt Channel between Buck Key and Captiva Island. Can carry 5' beyond marker G21 at half tide. Anchor where space permits. Can dinghy to Blind Pass and beaches. Resort Marina near G19. For $10 day you can use resort facilities. (#5,9,25)

Mile 13.1, {2.1}, Captiva Island, (323141): From ICW marker R38 go west as far as draft permits. (#25)

Mile 18.5, {2.1}, Cayo Costa, (322141): From ICW marker R50 head west towards the SE tip of Cayo Costa Island. Anchor as close to cove as draft permits. Entire island is a state park. Dinghy ashore and walk the beaches, swim or shell. (#25)

Mile 21.6, {2.1}, Useppa Island, (323141): From ICW marker R60 head NE to west side of Useppa Island. Sound in as close as draft permits. (#5,25)

Mile 23.1, {2.1}, Punta Blanca Island, (444441): Leave ICW halfway between marker G65 and G67 and proceed west to SE end of Punta Blanca Island. Stay close to end of island and follow shore around into protected pocket. Can carry 5' into anchorage. Anchor "med style"; stern to mangroves on island and anchor away from shore. Room for 6-8 boats. Can dinghy to Cayo Costa Park.

Mile 25, {2.1}, Pelican Bay, (333441): From ICW marker R72 head for south end of sand spit, about 235M. Best water is about 100 yards off sand bar. Note that shoals extend from both shores and tend to overlap a little. Once past bar, run parallel to shore slightly to right of center in 5-6'. Well beyond park dock is a pocket of deeper water for anchoring. Very popular. Take dinghy to shore and visit park and walk trails. $2/family honor system. (#25)

Mile 26, {1.9}, Punta Gorda: 20 miles NE of mile 26 on Charlotte Harbor is Fisherman's Village. This is a very popular marina for boats to winter. $9/ft/mo plus $50 liveaboard fee. Close to shopping. (#25)

Mile 28.5, {1.7}, Boca Grande, (444433): At ICW marker R2 head NW to G1 on Boca Grande Channel. Turn to starboard at G7 as you come into channel. 5 ½ ' at LW at entrance, but found 9-10' between channel and bridge. Anchor "med style"; stern tied to mangroves and anchor on bow. Dinghy to Pink Elephant and visit small seaside tourist community. (#25)

Mile 34.2, {1.6}, Boca Grande Swing Bridge-**VHF 09** (9'), **Restricted**: Jan 1 to May 31 7AM to 5PM opens every 15 minutes starting on the hour. (#19,21,22,24)

Mile 36, {1.6}, Cape Haze, (434322): From ICW marker R30 head NE into cove off Cape Haze. Anchor in 8-10'. Dinghy to bridge on canal off north side of cove and tie up. PO within walking distance. (#5,25)

Mile 39, {1.5}: Frequent car ferry crossing. (#5)

Mile 43.3, {1.6}, Englewood Beach, (333232): Halfway between marker R22 and bridge turn west crossing 5 ½' shoal into deeper white water. Favor shore to starboard near entrance. Then work towards the deeper water on port and avoid the sand bar correctly shown on chart. Anchor for wind protection of your choosing. Restaurant and dive shop short dinghy ride away. (#5,22,25)

Mile 43.5, {1.6}, Tom Adams Key Bridge-**VHF 09** (24'): On demand. (#5,22,24)

Mile 49.8, {1.6}, Manasota Bridge-**VHF 09** (24'): On demand. (#5,22)

Mile 55, {1.6}, South Venice Bridge-**VHF 09** (25'), **Restricted:** Saturday and Sunday only opens every 15 minutes. On demand rest of the time. (#5,22,24)

Mile 56.6, {1.6}, Venice Avenue Bridge-**VHF 09** (30'), **Restricted**: M-F 7AM to 4:30PM opens at 10, 30, and 50 minutes past the hour. Closed 4:35PM to 5:35PM. On demand all other times including weekends and holidays. (#5,22)

Mile 56.9, {1.6}, Hatchett Creek Bridge-**VHF 09** (16'), **Restricted**: M-F 7AM to 4:20PM opens every 20 minutes starting on the hour. Closed 4:25PM to 5:25PM. Weekends and holidays 7:30AM to 6PM opens every 15 minutes starting on the hour. On demand all other times. (#5,22)

Mile 58, {1.6}, Venice, (333222): Follow marked channel to Venice Yacht Club. Two options:
  (1) Anchor in 6' just north of Yacht Club. Reported shoaling to less than 6'.
  (2) **Free dock:** Free city dockage for 18 hours for 4 to 5 boats (433222) at Higel Marine Park next to VYC. Park has toilet, picnic tables and grill. One mile to convenience store. (#5)

Mile 59, {1.6}, Albee Bridge-**VHF 09** (14'): On demand. (#5,22)

Mile 63, {1.6}, Blackburn Bridge-**VHF 09** (9'): On demand. (#5,22)

Mile 67.5, {1.6}, White Beach, (333221): Between G55 and G57 go west towards shore and behind spit. Found constant 6' close to "white beach" shore and "spit". (#17)

Mile 68, {1.6}, Stickney Point Bridge-**VHF 09** (18'): On demand. (#5,22)

Mile 71.8, {1.6}, Siesta Key Bridge-**VHF 09** (25'), **Restricted**: Opens every 20 minutes starting on the hour. (#22)

Mile 73.4, {1.6}, Sarasota, (444433): Turn east off ICW between marker R8A and R10 and follow channel towards Jack's Marina, now called Marina Operations. Anchor north of Marina Operations near large silver building. Dinghy to marina to go ashore and shop. Dinghy fee $1 payable at the restaurant. (#18,22,25)

Mile 73.5, {1.6}, Ringling Causeway Bridge-**VHF 09** (22'), **Restricted**: 7AM to 6PM opens on the hour and half-hour. (#5,22)

Mile 84.9, {1.8}, Longboat Key, (322123): Leave ICW north of G39 and head west into anchorage south of Longboat Key Inlet. Anchor in 8-12' close to island. Popular and crowded on weekends. There is a dinghy dock and small shopping center south of Longboat Key. Millers restaurant has free dockage with dinner. (#25)

Mile 87.1, {1.8}, Cortez Bridge, (423322): Turn west off ICW south of Cortez Bridge at G49 and anchor in 5-8'. (#22)

Mile 87.2, {1.8}, Cortez Bridge-**VHF 09** (22'), **Restricted**: 7AM to 6PM opens on the hour and every 20 minutes thereafter. (5,18,22,24)

Mile 89.2, {1.8}, Anna Maria Bridge-**VHF 09** (25'), **Restricted**: 7AM to 6PM opens on the hour and every 20 minutes thereafter. (5,18,22,24)

Mile 93, {1.8}, Manatee River, (324131): Leave ICW at mile 93 and head east to marker R2 of Manatee River. Follow channel to marker R12 and turn to west into pocket behind Desoto Point. Sound your way in and watch for shoal shown on chart. Anchor in 7-8' and take dinghy to shore to visit Desoto National Memorial Park. Park has film on Desoto (free) and well-marked nature trails.

Mile 106, {2.3}, St. Petersburg, (334323): Proceed north 6 miles from R4 and enter the north Yacht Basin, just north of St. Petersburg pier. Anchor in 8-10'. Numerous sailboat activities on weekends. (#5,18)

Mile 110.5, {1.8}, Maximo Point Bridge-**VHF 09** (21'), **Restricted**: 7AM to 8PM opens on hour and half-hour.

Mile 113, {1.8}, Tierra Verde Bridge-**VHF 09** (25'), **Restricted**: Weekend and Holidays 9AM to 6PM opens every 15 minutes starting on the hour. (#22)

Mile 114, {1.8}, Vina Del Mar Bridge-**VHF 09** (25'), **Restricted**: Weekends and Holidays 7AM to 7PM opens on the hour and every 20 minutes thereafter. (#22)

Mile 116, {1.6}, Gulfport Municipal Marina: Leave ICW at G31 and follow Cats Point Channel to R14. Just before R14 head NE to Gulfport Marina Channel. Dockage $.50/ft. Shopping center 1 ½ mile walk.

Mile 117.7, {1.6}, Corey Causeway Bridge-**VHF09** (23'), **Restricted:** Opens on the hour and every 20 minutes thereafter. (#22)

Mile 119.0, {1.6}, Treasure Island Causeway Bridge-**VHF09** (8'), **Restricted:** Opens on the hour and every 15 minutes thereafter. (#22)

Mile 122.0, {1.6}, Welch Causeway Bridge-**VHF09** (25'), **Restricted:** Weekends and holidays opens on the hour and every 20 minutes thereafter. On demand weekdays. (#22)

Mile 126.0, {1.6}, Park Boulevard Bridge-**VHF09** (26'): Opens on demand. (#22)

Mile 129.0, {1.6}, Indian Rocks Beach Bridge-**VHF09** (25'): Opens on demand. (#22)

Mile 131.8, {1.6}, Belleair Causeway Bridge-**VHF09** (21'), **Restricted:** Weekends and holidays opens on the hour and every 15 minutes thereafter. On demand weekdays. (#22)

Mile 136.0, {1.6}, Clearwater Beach Bridge-**VHF09** (25'), **Restricted:** 9AM to 6PM opens on the hour and every 20 minutes thereafter. On demand other times. (#22)

Mile 141.7, {1.6}, Dunedin Bridge-**VHF09** (25'): Opens on demand. (#22)

Mile 141.8, {1.6}, Caladesi State Park (444441): Just south of Honeymoon Bridge, Turn west into the Honeymoon Island Channel. After ½ mile turn south at sign directing you to the Caladesi State Park Marina. Wonderful isolated marina. $8.88/night Jun 97.

CONTRIBUTORS

1. Bob and Elaine Reib aboard Snug, 36' Krogen trawler, 3' 6" draft.
2. Mark and Susanne Richter aboard Winnie The Pooh, custom 46' trawler, 4' 8" draft.
3. Jim and Kay Stolte aboard Siris IV, 36' Grand Banks trawler, 4' 6" draft.
4. Tim and Sharon Holock aboard Almost Perfection, 34' sailboat, 4' draft.
5. Ed and Marita Pyne aboard Marita, 36' Grand Banks trawler, 4' draft
6. August 1998 Chesapeake Bay Magazine
7. Dee Merian aboard 37' sailboat.
8. Ken McQuage aboard Mrs. Hudson, 36' Krogen trawler, 3' 6" draft.
9. Reade Tompson aboard 36' Allied Ketch, 4' 6" draft
10. Lang's Marina
11. Women Aboard Magazine
12. Bill and Judy Fletcher aboard Meander, 44' DeFever trawler, 5' draft.
13. Jan Willen Korthals aboard Iris, sailboat.
14. Fred and Betty Wright aboard Skookum Lady, 36' Cascade sloop, 6' draft.
15. Ann and Rob Blood aboard Cool Change, 26' sailboat, 2' 6" draft.
16. Vic and Lee Cooper aboard Meander, 42' Grand Banks trawler, 4' 6" draft.
17. Pete and Lesley Jarrett aboard Cloud Nine, 27' Mirage sailboat.
18. Russ and Tira Dreyfus aboard Pastis.
19. Bob and Colleen Pruitt aboard Long Shot, 36' Marine Trader, 4' draft.
20. Curt and Sue Dunham aboard Velvet, 36' Krogen trawler, 3' 6" draft.
21. Sandy and Bob Erskine aboard Sabo, 42' Krogen trawler, 4' 6" draft.
22. Dave and Karen Graham aboard Lisa Morgan, 41' DeFever trawler, 4' draft.
23. Bill and Dot Schuck aboard Sea Nest, 36' Albin trawler, 3' 6" draft.
24. Tom Murphy
25. Ed Ten Eyck, Jr aboard Norjac, 30' Cataline sailboat, 5' 3" draft.
26. Michael Briant aboard Bambola Quatre, 36' Moody sloop, 6' draft.
27. Bob and Judy Fout aboard Sans Souci
28. Anonymous

Appendix 1 - Fuel Prices

During a recent survey of marinas from the Hudson River to Fort Lauderdale, FL an effort was made to determine the best fuel prices along each stretch covered by this book. The complete listing of fuel prices and the dates of the survey are listed in *Marinas Along the Intracoastal Waterway*. It is important to note that fuel prices vary during the year. However, it has been my experience that as the fuel prices fluctuate up and down, the marinas with the lowest fuel prices on one day continue to be the marinas with the lowest fuel prices even when prices change. Likewise those marinas which charge the most, continue to charge the most.

Gasoline prices increased about 3 cents a gallon during the year and averaged $1.41/gal along the entire east coast. Prices are a little higher in NY ($1.47/gal) and lowest in VA, NC, and SC ($1.35).

Diesel, on the other hand fell in price about 5 cents per gallon, and varies widely within the reported area. Below I have listed the number of marinas surveyed in a given area, the lowest diesel price per gallon encountered and all marinas which charge within 5% of the lowest prices encountered. In addition, each marina listed below is highlighted in the appropriate section of this book. The price shown is for **100 gallons** of diesel fuel, paying **cash**. In some cases purchasing less than 100 gallons, you encounter a penalty of as much as $0.20/gal. Also, use of a credit card sometimes adds to the price shown. Finally, purchasing more than 200 gallons can reduce the price shown.

Hudson River - 155 miles

    No of marinas = 21   Average diesel price = $1.30   Lowest price = $1.16

    Best price = Mile 23.0 Shady Harbor marina diesel $1.19 & gasoline $1.35

                Mile 86.0 West Shore Marina diesel $1.16 & gasoline $1.50

                Mile 141.5 Englewood Boat Basin diesel $1.20 & gasoline $1.40

New Jersey - 115 miles

    No of marinas = 19   Average diesel price = $1.04   Lowest price = $0.90

    Best prices = Mile 4.6 Dale Yacht Basin diesel $0.94 & gasoline $1.30

                Mile 45.5 Beach Haven Yacht Club diesel $0.95 & gas $1.26

                Mile 109.0 Schooner Island Marina diesel $0.90 & gas $1.30

Delaware Bay & C&D Canal - 69 miles

    No of marinas = 4   Average diesel price = $1.02   Lowest price = $0.89

    Best prices = Mile 8.5 Summit North Marina diesel $0.89 & gas $1.40

              Mile13.9 Schaefer's Marina diesel $0.89 & gas $1.45

Anchorages Along the Intracoastal Waterway
Appendix 1 - Fuel prices

Chesapeake Bay MD - 207 miles
    No of marinas = 36   Average diesel price = $0.94   Lowest price = $0.76
    Best price =   Mile 53.0 Annapolis City Marina diesel $0.81 & gas $1.46
                Mile 67.6 Knapps Narrows Marina diesel $0.76 & gas $1.32
                Mile 97.5 Spring Cove Marina diesel $0.80 & gas $1.28
                Mile 139.0 Somers Cove Marina diesel $0.79 & gas $1.29

Virginia ICW – 30 miles
    No of marinas = 4   Average diesel price = $0.74   Lowest price = $0.70
    Best prices =   Mile 15.2 Centerville Waterway Marina diesel $0.88 & gas $1.34
                Mile 28.4 Pungo Ferry Marina diesel $0.70 & gas $1.27

North Carolina ICW - 321 miles
    No of marinas = 28   Average diesel price = $0.84   Lowest price = $0.59
    Best prices = Mile   49.5 Midway Marina diesel = $0.65 & gas $1.35
                Mile   49.6 Coinjock Marina diesel = $0.65 & gas $1.35
                Mile   49.6 Harrison's Marina diesel = $0.65 & gas $1.35
                Mile   84.1 Alligator River Marina diesel = $0.65 & gas $1.35
                Mile 246.9 New River Marina diesel = $0.59 & gas $1.10

South Carolina ICW - 240 miles
    No of marinas = 34   Average diesel price = $0.87   Lowest diesel = $0.70
    Best prices =   Mile 347.0 Anchor Marina diesel $0.75 & gas $1.25
                Mile 469.3 Ashley Marina diesel $0.75 & gas $1.32
                Mile 556.5 Outdoor Resorts Marina diesel $0.70 & gas $1.49
                Mile 563.7 Shelter Cove Marina $0.75 & gas $1.35

Georgia ICW - 136 miles
    No of marinas = 10   Average diesel price = $0.94   Lowest price = $0.74
    Best price =   Mile 680.0 Brunswick Landing diesel $0.74 & gas $1.23

Florida ICW - 350 miles
    No of marinas = 66   Average diesel price = $1.02   Lowest price = $0.72
    Best prices = Mile 716.4 Florida Petroleum diesel $0.73
                Mile 803.2 Palm Coast Marina diesel $0.76 & gas $1.40
                Mile 965.6 Port Petroleum diesel $0.72 & gas $1.33

Okeechobee Waterway – 146 miles
    No of marinas = 8   Average diesel price = $0.98   Lowest price = $0.84
    Best prices =   Mile 29.4 Indiantown Marina diesel $0.90 & gas $1.48
                Mile 155.2 Deep Lagoon Boat Club diesel $0.84 & gas $1.55

Appendix 2 - Do-It-Yourself Yards

Area 1 - Hudson River

Mile	Name	Lift
88.0	Whites Hudson River Marina	25T
116.5	Haverstraw Marina	25T
125.1	Julius Petersen	60T
149.5	Port Imperial Marina	35T
153.7	Liberty Harbor Marina	60T

Area 2 - New Jersey

Mile	Name	Lift
6.2	Winter Yacht Basin	50T
84.5	All Seasons Marina	
97.5	Avalon Point Marina	70T
101.9	Stone Harbor Marina	30T
114.0	Utsch's Marina	35T
114.0	Canyon Club Resort Marina	60T
114.2	Cape May Marina	25T

Area 3 - Delaware Bay

Mile	Name	Lift
34.0	Greenwich Boat Works	75T
53.9	Penn Salem Marina	35T

Area 4 - C&D Canal

Mile	Name	Lift
8.5	Summit North Marina	50T

Area 5 - Chesapeake Bay

Mile	Name	Lift
12.8	Charlestown Marina	50T
18.2	Georgetown Yacht Basin/Granar	110T
38.4	Baltimore Marine Center	55T
42.3	Scott Marine Service	25T
42.3	Lippincott Marina	25T
49.6	Chesapeake Bay Bridge Marina	70T
53.0	Bert Jabin's Yacht Yard #2	35T
53.0	Bert Jabin's Yacht Yard #1	35T
67.6	Herrington Harbour North	
67.6	Knapps Narrows Marina	35T

Area 5 - Chesapeake Bay

Mile	Name	Lift
81.2	Gateway Marina	15T
81.2	Yacht Maintenance Company	60T
81.2	Cambridge Marine	30T
97.5	Washburn's Boat Yard	35T
97.5	Spring Cove Marina	35T
139.0	Sea Mark Marine	50T
152.6	Norview Marina	30T
152.6	Walden's Marina	35T
152.6	Dozier Marine Center	50T
152.6	Chesapeake Cove	30T
152.6	Norton Yacht Sales	35T
152.6	Deltaville Marina	35T
152.6	Fishing Bay Harbor Marina	25T
191.8	Cobb's Marina	50T
191.8	Little Creek Marina	50T
191.8	Cutty Sark Marina	50T
191.8	Bay Marine	35T

Area 7 - Virginia ICW

Mile	Name	Lift
28.4	Pungo Ferry Marina	70T

Area 8 - North Carolina ICW

Mile	Name	Lift
135.7	Robb's Boatyard & Marina	75T
181.0	Deaton Yacht Service	30T
195.8	Bock Marine Builders	60T
228.4	Dudley's Marina	25T
246.8	Swan Point Marina	40T
288.1	Masonboro Boat Yard and Marin	19T
309.3	Southport Marina	75T

Area 9 - South Carolina ICW

Mile	Name	Lift
347.0	Anchor Marina	35T
476.1	Ross Marine	70T

Area   9 - South Carolina ICW

Mile	Name	Lift
563.7	Palmetto Bay Marina	50T

Area   10 - Georgia ICW

Mile	Name	Lift
582.0	Tidewater Boat Works	40T
583.2	Palmer Johnson Marina	100T
680.0	Brunswick Landing	50T

Area   11 - Florida ICW

Mile	Name	Lift
779.9	St. Augustine Marine	75T
835.2	Seven Seas Marina & Boatyard	30T
839.6	Lighthouse Boat Works	70T
878.1	Westland Marine	40T
893.6	Harbortown Marina.	70T
897.3	Whitley Marine	37T
897.5	Indian Cove Marina	25T
933.9	Sebastian River Marina	40T
964.1	Riverside Marina and Boat Work	70T
965.1	Cracker Boy Boat Works	50T
965.1	Harbortown Marina	150T
981.8	Anchor's Aweigh Marine	40T
987.8	Top Side Marina	35T
987.8	Port Salerno Marine	25T
1011.7	Ways, The	70T
1017.4	New Port Cove Marine Center	60T
1017.9	Old Slip Marine	25T
1018.1	Cracker Boy Boat Works South	110T
1019.8	Rybovich Spencer	125T
1030.4	Murrelle Marina	30T
1032.5	Palm Beach Yacht Center	70T
1195.0	Marathon Marina and Boat Yard	25T

Area   12 - Okeechobee

Mile	Name	Lift
6.8	St. Lucie Marine	30T
29.4	Indiantown Marina	25T
89.0	Glades Boat Storage	40T

Area   13 - Florida SW Coast

Mile	Name	Lift
4.6	Compass Rose Marina	35T